PERSPECTIVES

Digital Transformation Through the Lens of Strategic Marketing

Lynn M. Scheurell

Download Your Free Digital Transformation Blueprint

A downloadable PDF that breaks down the five steps of developing and delivering Savvier brand experiences.

Get It NOW at
savvyx.com/blueprint/

MIZRAHI PRESS

Perspectives:
Digital Transformation Through the Lens of Strategic Marketing

ISBN-13: 978-0-9801550-5-1 (paperback)

Published by Mizrahi Press
A Division of Creative Catalyst LLC
MyCreativeCatalyst.com

Thank you to my clients and employers for the opportunity to explore the vast subject of digital transformation. I appreciate those who contribute their work and expertise in helping companies and their people achieve next-level business outcomes through technology—and for sharing your experiences with me.

Endorsements

"Lynn is the most brilliant marketing and tech writer on the planet. She absorbs information so quickly, and she delivers perfect copy. In my experience, no one can develop, conceptualize, communicate, and refine brand messaging better than Lynn. She meets and exceeds all deadlines and works entirely from passion and personal motivation. Lynn also works well in a group, inspiring new ideas, and helping the team reach common, concise goals. Uniquely, Lynn's can transition from blogs, to press releases, to documentation and novels and long-form writing. She is an exceptional copywriter as well and can correct and refresh legacy content into a modern voice. Lynn is devoted and loyal, with an uplifting attitude that inspires confidence."

~ Christopher Justice, CEO

"Lynn is an exceptional writer, content marketer and digital strategist but what makes her really stand out is her high degree of EI (emotional intelligence) and her passion for people. She is an expert in human behavior and enrolling people towards a vision, a digital transformation initiative or any other change management process comes easy and is a natural part of her leadership. Lynn's "human" touch makes her a strong and modern leader. I highly recommend her to any company looking for change, innovation, or development of any kind."

~ Jessica Sundstrom,
Chief Commercial Officer and
Chief Marketing Officer

Table of Contents

Who Am I and Why Trust Me?

When I was about seventeen, I had my first crisis of meaning. What was I supposed to study? What degree should I get? What was I supposed to DO with my life? I talked to guidance counselors, teachers, parents, store clerks, librarians and anybody standing still who might have an idea for me. I took multiple aptitude tests to find out what I was good at (including for the military but that's another story). Despite all my searching, I did not get any answers that felt right. It was frustrating. From my perspective, I was determining the course of the rest of my life and I wanted to do it RIGHT.

One morning while in bed between sleep and waking, I heard a voice. Nobody was there with me—but I distinctly heard a voice. It said, "actualize potential." What? I sat up to sort it out. The only clarity I had was a feeling around those words—they felt RIGHT. In that moment, I understood that my unique purpose was to actualize potential.

Over the course of my life, that proved to be where I am most comfortable—in being a catalyst for transformation. It started with friends and spread to acquaintances, then to people I would meet standing in lines, and then to colleagues. I found I had a talent for insight when it came to seeing current circumstances and identifying possibilities from it, then how to turn them into reality.

Professionally, I had a variety of jobs—everything from to ballroom dance instructor to restaurant manager to physician recruiter to temp agency manager—along with my own business born from people

1

insisting they pay me for my clarity. Eventually, I formalized that into a consultancy of sorts, working with entrepreneurs and business owners through various aspects of business-building. I became known for helping my clients accelerate their outcomes through a variety of tools and, more significantly, compelling clarity.

My clients have always said I bring an energy that infuses them with inspiration, and a perspective they couldn't see on their own. I love that. As we worked together, they would ask me to turn my clarity into narrative form for them to use in their marketing. That turned into helping them build their websites, which led me into the world of internet marketing. Somehow, I received a Woman in Ecommerce award. And I attracted enough business to keep me afloat financially as I stumbled around figuring out my system for creating transformation by working with my clients.

Naturally, whatever I learned for myself became part of what I could share with others to compress their learning curve. I didn't want others to go through the confusion, overwhelm and dissatisfaction of not knowing that I had experienced.

At one point, having spent a healthy $50,000 on building my skills portfolio, things were not going all that great in my business. In that moment, a dear friend called and said he needed a writer, someone to churn out content without needing a lot of direction, available NOW. I was not about to take a job—at this point, I was committed to revitalizing my business. He nearly begged me to help him and said it would be only a few months; that turned into nearly a year and a half. That was when I discovered my abilities to create transformation applied to B2B environments as well.

My decades of experience in digital marketing, brand development, systems thinking, thought leadership and writing brought insight and articulation together for fresh results. Almost by accident, I discovered my life purpose of actualizing potential had a new playground—B2B digital transformation.

While my resume in the B2B space has only been a little more than six-ish years (at the time of this writing), and in the IT space, I've been honing the skills needed to guide and support digital transformation for decades. Even more, I was born for it. I am a catalyst, an accelerator, a transformationalist.

What to Expect In This Book

One of the afflictions of working in business is the feeling of 'never enough'—time, clients, content, pipeline, money, campaigns, form fills, etc. This leads to overwhelm, burn-out, fragmented initiatives, redundant effort and all kinds of dysfunctional gunk that clogs the path to meaningful outcomes. Digital transformation is the solution to 'never enough-ness'.

As a deceptively simple definition, digital transformation is the process of streamlining, prioritizing, and addressing systemic constraints to support delivering greater value effectively—with ease and efficiency—to both customers and employees. In other words, the results of digital transformation are less stress, increased productivity, and happy people.

For transparency, my process to initiate digital transformation is by way of marketing. Why? Because marketing is about positioning specific outcomes of value through a promise backed by data to gain support via either brand recognition or business (new and/or renewed). A good marketer understands and uses the best techniques to get optimal visibility with the right future customers; a great marketer introduces the leading edge for strategic advantage in gaining visibility both externally and internally.

My intention in writing this book is to share what I know about digital transformation so it isn't so daunting as a process for continuous improvement. I believe it's one of the most significant and essential priorities of our time. My secret dream is this book be a conversation-starter within organizations by sparking ideas through a shared reading experience. And I want to help companies around the world be more successful in taking on digital transformation by being a resource with what I know.

Secondly, a marketing brain seeks to find the opportunities to educate and deliver value to audiences. I don't get into campaign specifics or data nuts and bolts here… but I do reference how to strategically relate to digital transformation through a marketing perspective.

How to Get the Most from this Book

Following is what you need to know to get the most out of this book.

First, it's practical. I've found that ideas without strategy remain a vision (OR expend tremendous effort for not enough return), and vision without action never happens. I'm not an academic nor an economist so this is written for people like me who are leading and doing the work (or want to!). This book may give you what you need to create a business case or show you what you're already doing that is transformative for your company.

Second, it's about clarity. When you aren't clear, it's challenging to make next-level decisions. If you go for it anyway, you will accelerate outcomes—but they will likely not be what you wanted to create.

Third, it's about action. As said above, what you read here is meaningless if you don't start applying it, regardless of company vertical, annual revenues or life stage. Take the nuggets you get and think about how they relate to your company; write them down for reference so you can come back to them later during strategic planning.

Fourth, it's about connection. This book is designed to be a firestarter for conversations, both within your company and between you and I. This is about exploring ideas, developing trust, getting to know each other a bit and, ultimately, help us decide if we will work together someday.

Fifth, it's about strategic marketing. That is a play on words, by the way, because you are marketing digital transformation as a benefit to both external (customers, partners, stakeholders) AND internal audiences (leadership, employees). This is not about the intricacies of techniques because you can get those anywhere. Instead, by showing you how to identify and articulate the opportunities for digital transformation in your organization, you can build a case and gain buy-in for the value of a digital transformation initiative in your company.

~ ~ ~ ~

Personally, I am committed to helping you serve more clients and customers through your organization. And I do work with organizations to work through digital transformation; if that could be helpful to you, please send me an email or find me on social media so we can connect and explore together.

Meanwhile, if you like what you get from this book, I would love to hear from you. I want to know you and your business, and learn what your takeaway(s) was from reading this book. Please post your thoughts on my LinkedIn page at **linkedin.com/in/lynnscheurell/**. Thanks in advance!

It's an honor for me to be your Catalyst in digital transformation. The time is now to determine, then activate, what's needed to deliver greater value to your customers and employees as an organization. It's really the only target worth having because such a triple-win—for your organization, customers, and employees—means profit will be a natural outcome.

Here's to digital transformation—and all it can bring your organization!

—Lynn Scheurell

The Experience Economy

To start at the beginning, digital transformation is a process to deliver value in today's Experience Economy. Customers and users (employees, stakeholders, partners) are savvier, more informed and increasingly empowered today than ever—they drive enterprise and determine the fate of businesses today.

While I shared this simple definition in the introduction, it's worth restating here because it sets the context for everything that follows. Digital transformation is the process of streamlining, prioritizing, and addressing systemic constraints to support delivering greater value effectively—with ease and efficiency—to both customers and employees. In other words, the results of digital transformation are less stress, increased productivity, and happy people.

What Is the Experience Economy?

The Experience Economy is all about the perception people gain as a result of their interaction with your brand and company—in short, their experience. And, naturally, their expectations are created based on their last great brand experience. (On behalf of enterprises everywhere, thanks Amazon.)

B2B is a reference to businesses that sell to business; however, the reality is business happens H2H—human to human—regardless of transaction size, audience, industry, or solution. The Experience Economy demands thoughtfully designed touchpoints to cultivate connection, trust, rapport, and, ultimately, action. When buyers have experienced enough value, they become customers.

When you deliver enough value to your audience(s) through their experience with your company's brand, profit is a natural and predictable by-product.

Industry and Digital Enterprise

The way business has been done historically no longer holds in this digital environment. For decades, as a result of the Industrial Revolution, business has operated off two assertions: 1) their customer is always external, and, 2) their customers fit in a box. This is the consequence of Henry Ford inventing the assembly line in 1913 for his cars. He reduced building a vehicle from 12+ hours to just 2.5 hours. That led to a process efficiency template that business claimed as well for the next century.

The issue is that the conveyor belt with identical parts is not a relevant model outside the manufacturing industry. While business today needs to create a predictable result, it is not about creating the same result for every customer. It is no longer efficient or desirable to think in linear terms about customer experience or satisfaction. The reality is today's customer expects personalized service based on where they are in their relationship with a brand; it's not about where the company thinks they should be in their experience.

Additionally, customer experience external paying customers AND internal staff, leaders, stakeholders, and partners. Marketers need to think through and deliver on tailored experiences for each of these audience(s) as well.

Three Trends Shaping Business Today

The following three trends are disruptions that will determine, ultimately, the competitive edge a company has in their market. By understanding the ramifications of these trends, you can strategically build trust, deliver greater value, and engage customers and users with personalized services to simplify their lives.

1. Everything Is an Experience

The number one driver of digital transformation is to be aware that everything connected to your brand is an experience that will either attract or repel positive attention and support from customers and users. Experience makes the intangible tangible for your customers and users. That includes customer experience, user experience, digital experience, employee experience, brand experience, ecommerce experience, and every other aspect of business that exists.

Every touchpoint with a brand sets the expectation for the next experience, regardless of the user's relationship with the brand. Brands are competing cross-industry for attention as the last experience from any company in any industry sets the pace and tone for the users of your organization's experience. The digital economy has levelled the playing field for enterprises regardless of size or brand recognition in their market.

Takeaway: The quality of experience your brand delivers sets the baseline for trust and future transactions throughout the buying journey. It requires integrated systems that talk to each other to share data for streamlined processes and a seamless experience for customers and users. Your brand's experience IS your brand in action.

2. Customers Are Savvy and Self-Sufficient

Buyers and future customers are more educated and empowered than ever through consuming information as research. They are increasingly using content—reviews, social proof, success stories, downloadable PDFs and more—to make buying decisions. Essentially, in-person sales are becoming digitally enabled in this new environment of buyer enablement. Your content must answer the questions buyers are asking about your solution. Resources, self-service education, marketing materials, and selling aids need to be accessible at buyers' convenience. The good news is you can glean actionable insights from your in-house data to know what content is most viewed, has highest conversions, and which would benefit from adding greater value in some way.

Takeaway: Buyers are intelligent and self-sufficient—they are relying on their own research to identify solutions to their problems. Enterprises need content strategies that account for customer preferences and behaviors, based on analyzing collected data. A brand's online presence should convey credibility, authority, and trust—while initiating selling conversations on-demand when buyers are ready to talk.

3. Invisible Technology Is the Standard

Buyers and customers expect, and should be able, to get what they need when they want it how they want—and it should just work. Nothing complicated. Everything needs to be intuitive so no involved training is needed. The Internet of Things has shifted and connected business like never before… marketplace audiences expect the entire range of their brand experience to be safe and personalize their experience.

Takeaway: Your solutions, connectivity, and processes must keep up with the pace of business and customer expectations throughout the business lifecycle. This all needs to happen concurrently with collecting, protecting, and accessing real-time data. IT systems need to integrate the use of leading-edge technology to automate where it makes sense, like with chatbots, machine-learning, and predictive analytics.

Combined, these three trends are the elements that create the formula for a company-wide digital transformation journey.

Experience = Content + Relevance + Accessibility

To deliver this formula successfully means having invisible technology, which means embarking on a digital transformation journey that integrates, unifies, and streamlines customer and user experiences, processes, and technology — insightfully, seamlessly, and invisibly.

The Power of Micro-Moments

Just like in the real world, business unfolds through their audiences' perception of it gained through experiencing it. Those experiences and perceptions are both within and outside a company's knowledge and ability to influence them. And yet, these perceptions shape how buyers and customers relate to that company.

In case that just bent your mind, think about a hotel stay… while a hotel can make certain commitments to guests, the actual experience for any guest is created in the moment and considers all factors (like, other guests, equipment malfunctions, big parties on property, etc.). The exact intangible deliverable cannot be guaranteed nor experienced prior to it happening; the ultimate perception of that hotel brand will be determined to some degree through that experience as it unfolds.

Every mention or touchpoint with a brand, whether self-generated or user-generated—becomes part of that brand's experience. That means a casual conversation in passing to an online review to social chatter online can all impact a brand. Ironically, a brand may not even know their own story if a perception or experience has been shared without their knowledge or ability to find or manage it. Again, the Experience Economy puts the control of a brand's success (or obsoletion) in the hands of customers, who make their assessment from micro-moment encounters with that brand.

Historically, enterprise has used Ford's assembly line as a model to progress customer relationships. That means marketers have been conditioned to think in similar end-product results for every customer.

Even more, businesses have traditionally determined the best out-comes for the customers vs. allowing the customer's preferences and needs drive the relationship. Once these results have been determined, and the assembly line in motion, the consumers of the brand prom-ise—including staff and leaders, along with infrastructure, workflows, technology, and standards, have all operated with that same linear, industrial model of business. This means enterprise uses a 100-year old blueprint as the compass for conducting business in today's digi-tally-shrewd environment.

The workers who deliver products and services do so using the best practices they've been taught. The buyers of those goods are speaking up and voting with their money about what they want; brand loyalty is transient as customers drive business now. Given that buyers and customers have more options than ever as a result of accessible infor-mation delivered via technology, business leaders likely do not know how to reclaim the proverbial (traditional) reins. In other words, what got business 'here' will not get today's business 'there'.

To be successful today, business must adapt to dynamic market con-ditions and conversations by making real-time shifts in offers, cam-paigns, and processes while delivering predictable, relevant value through personalized relationships.

Ecosystems, Innovation and Enterprise

Ecosystems define the cycle of life, from an Amazonian jungle to what's happening in the world of your buyers and customers. Understanding the ecosystem of your brand experience, through the eyes of your audience(s), is the key to creating successful connections. For example, the Internet of Things (IoT) means a customer can order a ride from their wrist and their refrigerator can create their grocery shopping list. Buyers and customers interpret this digital capability into the "Internet of Me"—essentially, a personal ecosystem.

Accordingly, organizations must answer one question to ensure sustainability and market differentiation:

Is your company capable and ready to deliver seamless, frictionless, personalized customer- and user-centric experiences?

As the term implies, an ecosystem is a system, or network, composed of individual parts that, through interdependent interaction, form a community. Smaller ecosystems join to create larger ecosystems. For example, algae is fish food, fish enrich water, which feeds plants that provide oxygen. Another example, people live in homes located in neighborhoods that become communities... light bulbs in houses are powered by local power plants that are connected to regional power grids that create a national network of electricity you can see from space... the people around a table who collaborate on a project that generates new opportunities and revenues by delivering value to customers that power a business and more. In short, ecosystems are everywhere.

What are Digital Ecosystems?

Since an ecosystem is a system, or a group of interconnected elements, formed by the interaction of a community of individual elements with their environment, a digital ecosystem is the confluence of human engagement, online brand presence, and technology (to name a few of the elements within). The ultimate outcome of digital transformation is a streamlined ecosystem, including supporting elements, into frictionless operations.

Buyer, customer, and user expectations and experiences are influenced by the ecosystems in which they participate. The ability to work with, and within, these ecosystems, as well as how integrated and streamlined your business makes these ecosystems, becomes a determining factor in your company's success.

If any part of your internal ecosystem is misaligned, it means your business is losing revenues, customers, opportunities, and the competitive edge—that's the natural law of enterprise. Meaning, when your company delivers better experiences and greater value through your ecosystem, you outpace your competition. The converse is also true... if your company does not deliver better experiences and greater value to your audience(s), your competitors will be happy to do so.

Given the IoT, brand experiences are measured by and compete with the last best experience a customer had with any company. Maturity, size, vertical market... none of these matters—only customer perception of smooth, relevant, valuable delivery matters. Is Ikea doing something amazing? How about Dell or Canon or Amazon or Apple or one of the big banks or a major healthcare system? Those are now the benchmarks by which your customers are evaluating their experience with your brand.

Ecosystem priorities center around members' concerns, from buying groceries to getting insurance to booking a pet sitter and more. Success brands make these priorities happen faster, easier, cheaper, smoother. (And where that doesn't happen, or worse, if the brand breaks trust, customers vote with their dollars.)

Each brand and buying experience become an ecosystem within the customer's ecosystem. This might be the secret to capitalism—if your brand ecosystem is better than anybody else's brand ecosystem, yours gets to live in your customer's ecosystem.

The Buying Journey and the Brand Ecosystem

Here's what is happening for customers when they are buying a solution to solve a problem or meet a need. That customer first becomes aware of their need and looks to find a solution. Once they identify a potential solution, they evaluate through some sort of trial. When they have a successful experience, they buy and start using the solution. Lastly, when they're successful because of that solution, they want to share how they did it so they become brand advocates. That's what we enterprise folk would call nirvana.

Anyway, this is the customer buying journey. Once the customer becomes an advocate, you still have to continue to earn their business and be worthy of their trust. So you don't get to nirvana and coast... remember, nobody gets to coast now.

The customer determines the value of a brand as a solution provider. Meaning, the company is continuously adjusting to meet buyer, customer, and user perceptions even as the company maintains systems, workflows, structures, and processes.

In terms of business, ecosystems are based around the customer (while customer ecosystems do consider company ecosystems). Business ecosystems include everything from transactional procedures to supporting employee performance to regulatory compliance to partner relations to servicing customer concerns to keeping technology current to monitoring the market and seeing the future to innovate solutions and more.

Note that business ecosystems revolve around both external customers and internal users (staff and leaders). Customer revenues create cash flow, while employees are vital to keeping the doors open—both must be satisfied for the company to be profitable. Internal company ecosystems should be designed to extend relationships and reduce the need for attraction (or recruiting). Note: companies must support and facilitate employees in operating at peak levels to deliver value; coasting on past successes or traditional status quo is no longer an option to remain competitive.

Anyway, a lot of this is behind the scenes as customers and users don't see all that goes into the business ecosystem. Also, this does not include Artificial Intelligence (AI) or 3D printing or virtual reality or any of the fast-developing technologies that are going to have a big impact on business in the future. This is just focusing on what is working now.

In the largest picture, the overall business ecosystem considers, not only its own structures, processes, and considerations but the customers' ecosystems and buying journey as well. The pressure is on the business because it must seamlessly meet the customer where they are in their buying journey to cultivate a relationship. And that happens through using current technology to collect and share data, which must then be converted into actionable insights. If, at any point, the business infrastructure is outdated or insufficient, the entire ecosystem is potentially at risk. Companies need to continuously assess and upgrade their ecosystem(s) to stay current and competitive.

Seven Ways to Assess Your Ecosystem

There are seven ways to assess how your brand is doing in terms of preparing for and delivering a great customer experience from within your current ecosystem.

1. Meet Real-Time Demands

Business happens fast—and brands need to not only respond but anticipate faster to meet informed customer expectations and needs. Business departments—marketing, business development, customer relationship managers, customer experience managers—need real-time information to be as proactive and responsive as possible. Key decisions need to be made by leaders, often on the fly, for business growth. Data and the ability to interpret it in real-time is necessary for successful business in today's digital environment.

2. Clean Data

Data is the key to success through the business insights, decisions and actions that rely on it. Data should be clean, usable, and integrated, regardless of source. Naturally, customer privacy should be considered in all data protocols.

3. Consistently Awesome Brand Experience

Customer experience is the unique and, in reality, only sustainable business advantage in today's business landscape. It's not just what and how you do what you do but how your customers perceive and experience your brand that defines your customer experience. Naturally, your company needs to have solid capabilities, evolving solutions, and strong customer relationships. Beyond that, your brand needs to be visible across different channels and consistently awesome, whatever the touchpoint, access device, location, or time of day.

4. Cloud Technologies

Cloud-based technologies give your company scalability that flexes with business usage and needs. One benefit is that companies pay only for what they use; other benefits include not having to budget, purchase or maintain servers, including staff time to install, maintain, and upgrade. Cloud-based technologies are always current and, due to rapid deployment capabilities, customers and users will always enjoy the most current experience.

5. Peak Performance

As mentioned earlier, external customers are not the only customers of your organization—so are your staff. Users need to be able to do their jobs without friction, meaning from any device, anywhere, any time—so the organization gets the full benefit of their contributions. Systems should be intuitive to use and easy to access to minimize, or even eliminate, any learning curve. Users need to be able to collaborate easily, without worrying about version control or getting into systems without proper security and permissions. Processes need to support users in contributing their best work vs. using workarounds or being frustrated with systems. Employee workflows, permission, and processes should be user-friendly and frictionless.

6. Agile Technology

Agility in systems means your company can flex to meet emerging opportunities. Apps, processes, and data should link into the larger network, or ecosystem, to evolve with business growth. Technology should scale to serve on demand as business grows. Your company should be able to innovate and deploy new solutions to meet dynamic customer conversations. Without agility, your company is poised to be out-paced by your competitors.

7. Cohesive Data

When data is not integrated and, therefore, fragmented, it can cost your company in opportunities, customers, revenues, partners and even employees. Companies must have unified communications and a complete picture of what's happening throughout the organization. Streamlined systems save time and minimize the potential for human error and ensure cohesive data throughout the company. Connecting data sources so they talk to each other is an essential upshift for all business ecosystems.

The Ecosystem of Technology

There are many ecosystems within an organization that need their own flavor of attention. That said, the obvious ecosystem of technology is usually the first thought that arises when thinking about digital transformation.

Technology initiates through a demand for data in some way— maybe an imminent go to market offer, reinventing a customer experience, initiating a campaign or something else. When your company's IT systems are outdated, your organization is lacking the agility needed to meet real-time demands, which can compromise your organization's ability to conduct business in today's digital business environment.

Technology alone cannot deliver on demand. Whatever the technology, it needs to be implemented and integrated with current IT infrastructure. Quality implementation requires understanding the business goals as well as applying expertise to the implementation process. There also must be consideration given to change management for people.

Therefore, digital transformation is about combining technology with implementation expertise and change management (both for people and processes) to empower data exchange, usability, and intelligence for decision-making.

Companies now must have their DNA (Digital Niche Advantage) in play. That is typically the domain of marketing, although the sales function is on the same continuum as marketing for messaging and should be fluent in that conversation as well. The questions now are: can they scale, lead their industry, and anticipate customer needs to innovate solutions?

Next-Level Business Requires (Digital) Transformation

As already shared, it's not business-as-usual anymore—it's business as customers drive it. Accordingly, enterprises today need to upshift people, processes, and profit centers to be customer driven. It's about innovating new solutions and protocols while being predictively responsive. The process to accomplish this—to stay ahead of customer needs and demands and retain a competitive edge—is digital transformation.

Business is not just about the transaction that occurs but, more importantly, the relationships within that transaction as well. These relationships are facilitated by technology automating routine tasks and personalizing communications by applying insights gleaned from data. The result is that employees are supported for their peak performance, especially in building connections with customers (and their colleagues).

As this happens, technology will become more 'ambient'—just part of the background that is unobtrusive but ever-present. It will be integrated into and across customer and user experiences. And mass personalization will become more sophisticated, and the domain of staff with specialized skills. New products, services, and processes will be developed based on opportunities we can't yet see today as well as dynamic market conversations.

This is the backdrop, the context, of next-level business success. It becomes easy to see why 'digital transformation' became the buzz phrase for a much larger, all-encompassing, organization-wide process that can change everything for a company or even industry.

At this point, organizations are at a proverbial crossroads. They can choose to respond to the call of market conditions in one-off scenarios OR they can proactively disrupt their own systems to innovate better value delivery which, naturally, initiates digital transformation.

Symptoms That Digital Transformation Is Needed

There are many symptoms that indicate whether a company needs to upshift its capacity for delivering value in today's increasingly fast-paced business landscape. Symptoms are not typically singular; instead, just one can be a red flag to existing systemic issues.

Any one of those symptoms—and there may be others—indicates it's time for your organization to consider new options for delivering greater value in the Experience Economy. Your company's future depends on it.

See table of symptoms on following pages.

Symptoms That Precede Need for Digital Transformation

Planning to plan (vs. actually planning)	Not knowing the market (or current conversations)	Inconsistently managing social presence
Barriers to collaboration	Not able to articulate their differentiator	Not establishing or adhering to brand-wide standards and practices
Inefficient (reactive) communications	Lacking focus (goals / targets)	Not maintaining consistent voice and personality across channels
Fragmented martech stack	Not knowing what content to create and promote	Not demonstrating ROI (or figuring out how to)
Legacy systems (teams, technology, workflows)	Not driving quality leads	Not determining what metrics to monitor
Functional silos (between sales & marketing & IT, for example)	Promoting brand awareness poorly in a saturated environment	Not managing continuously incoming data
Erratic knowledge transfer	Not recruiting or finding quality content generators	Not optimizing brand / messaging across channels
C-suite separation from front lines	Not holding others accountable / having performance standards	Not engaging with customers in authentic conversations (only posting/promoting)
Employee disenfranchisement	Postponing or delaying response to customer conversations	Not identifying internal transformation champions
Not resourcing right/ quality talent as needed	Not targeting ideal customers within marketplace	Not staying current w/ industry news, technology, best practices

Symptoms That Precede Need for Digital Transformation (continued)

Not beginning enterprise-wide transformation process (or knowing how to)	Not owning the (right) conversation socially	Not educating employees on marketing and brand management
Misunderstanding customer emotional buying triggers	Not innovating mindset, workflows and customer solutions	Not managing online reputation
Not plotting customer lifecycles to intentional touchpoints	Systems incompatibility and/or lengthy integrations	Not optimizing campaigns
Not visioning the future to both accommodate and lead the path to it	Lacking career training and career path development	Not being transparent, especially when handling problems

Companies typically try to model what others are doing but try to do it faster, cheaper, smarter, longer than everyone else but still expecting fresh, personalized outcomes. This is proverbial insanity—doing the same thing repeatedly while expecting different results. That's where digital transformation comes into the picture—it's a personalized approach to optimizing your organization's value delivery system(s).

What Established Organizations Need to Know

Established organizations with deep roots in doing what they do will naturally be slower to change, even if triggered to do so by a significant industry or market disruption. That's not a criticism—merely a reality because there are more moving parts. However, the market doesn't wait—there are expectations from future and current customers, as well as competitors, that will dictate the pace of change.

In fact, the pressure for being an industry leader is likely heightened for established companies. They are perceived to have the resources to do what's needed to upgrade their systems, resources, brand presence, etc.

In all cases, marketing backed by technology is the bridge to established organizations' success in serving customers better in today's digital economy. Personalized touch points, humanizing the commerce journey, and being where the customer is already looking are key to the 'new' customer experience narrative. Next-level customer experience is about self-service capabilities, 'invisible' technology that just works, and predictive, personalized offers and solutions. To achieve that next-level customer experience, it becomes necessary to undertake digital transformation initiatives.

Disruption, Customer Experience and Opportunities

Companies cannot afford comfort zones anymore, which are the death knell in today's digital business environment. While there is always a dance between safety, security, stability and growth, the desire for predictable results can slow, or even stop, forward-moving momentum.

In other words, the desire for predictability, which is a basic life need, can create a collective perspective—a comfort zone around priorities, actions, workflows, and more—that lulls forward momentum, stalls innovation, and jeopardizes the company's future. Working through comfort zones affords companies next-level visibility, processes, and rewards in business.

Comfort zones, like the previously mentioned symptoms indicating the opportunity for digital transformation, can show up in different ways.

- Continuing to do things simply because they have always been done a particular way
- Accepting a skills vacuum that maintains status quo
- Winning 'now' supersedes long-term planning.
- Not scaling workflows, personnel, communications, and technologies appropriately.
- Allowing resistance to change to exist without being addressed to avoid challenging accepted beliefs.

- Purchasing decisions for tech are made without the IT team's knowledge (aka, "shadow IT").
- Not investing in unifying capabilities for the whole of the ecosystem (and, instead, buying one-off solutions)
- Not adopting (or delaying) the necessary mindset to navigate today's lean, fast-paced business environment.
- Ignoring or not investing in resources for innovation, company-wide upgrades, or digital transformation initiatives driven by the ideal customer needs, wants, behaviors, and preferences.

Proven methods are suffering obsolescence as dynamic market conversations and business circumstances unfold—missing a cue or lagging in acting on new information can jeopardize your company. Even one of the conditions in the Symptoms That Precede Need for Digital Transformation chart (previously shown) could indicate that transformation is needed on some level to remain competitive in your industry. The discomfort of transformation is essential to grow; the choice is whether a company is proactive or reactive about it.

In any initiative to transcend the status quo of comfort zones, there will be disruption. Such action is needed to surface what needs to be resolved as well as new opportunities for growth. Using your customer's delight as your compass will naturally illuminate the changes needed and ensure systems, processes, and paradigms will upshift appropriately.

Some examples of what it could look like to upshift comfort zones to better serve your customers can look like the following (and others):

- Explore what a significant bump in customer orders would do to your company's systems.
- Invite staff to shadow each other to learn what and why they do what they do to get results.

- Allow a certain amount of time for staff to innovate solutions, improve workflows, or upgrade systems for added customer value.
- Try systematically 'breaking' individual business units to intentionally create problems, then fix those breakdowns before customers experience them.
- Explore trends to project such outcomes as emerging opportunities, potential partnerships, and possible constrictions that need to be addressed in adapting to customer needs and wants.
- Host future customers as a sounding board group around key concepts to discover any questions or needed clarifications about your company's vision, offers, processes.
- Interview lost customers to learn their reasoning for not moving forward with your company's solution so you can refine according to those insights.
- Analyze competitors for marketing positioning, revenue model, and visibility strategies to identify customer trends, gaps in service, fresh opportunities, and ideas that could serve customers better.

Digital transformation, continuous growth, and deliberate improvement keep your organization on the leading edge with agility, relevance, and value-orientation. This is the only comfort zone worth having in business today.

Traditional vs. Transformed Approach

Transparency, authenticity, and clarity are the fabric of business visibility today. Business has evolved to make customer satisfaction the epicenter of culture, processes, and service. As a result, profit is a by-product vs. the only driver of operations.

Accordingly, the way customer experiences are shaped is different in today's market. Traditional marketing has been passive or 'push'—as in, a static brochure website or sending blast emails. Transformed marketing today is about 'pull' strategies that use personalized and targeted content based on customer preferences and behaviors. Marketers today use progressive profiling, journey mapping, geolocational promotions, mobile marketing and coordinated omnichannel presence to be in alignment with recommended best practices for digital marketing.

The need for digital transformation can begin with the CEO's mandate, the CMO's CX strategy, the CIO's implementation of upgrading IT, front-line staff, or leadership. Regardless of where transformation initiates, the organization as a whole will be affected. It is a significant undertaking and can be rigorous and, yet, without it, an organization could become obsolete. Digital transformation is the path to remaining viable in today's market.

Note: for our purposes in this book, CEO means Chief Executive Officer, CMO means Chief Marketing Officer, and CIO means Chief Information Officer (and includes CTO or any other technical leadership equivalent).

Disruption Surfaces New Opportunities

Disruption is an unexpected call to upshift for new growth. It's typically about something greater than the current circumstances, although it is an abrupt and usually unnerving way to receive a proverbial wake-up call. It changes plans, interrupts routine, shifts events… often it is unwanted or unexpected.

You can proactively cause disruption; at that point, it becomes innovation. That is the kind of thinking that positions companies to be an industry leader—because they have disrupted the status quo in their industry and displaced existing market leaders through their innovation. While counter-intuitive, disruption can be a positive force for change. Ultimately, disruption is always transformational.

Inherently, disruption invites upshifting which, for companies, means considering how customer experience is impacted. Customer experience, as already stated, is any company's unique differentiator and only sustainable advantage in business today. It's not about technical wizardry but about sincere connection with customers—and users—through every touch point. Each connection needs to be always-on to deliver personalized value and results on demand through the device of choice in the moment. Optimizing relationships means taking time and friction out of the equation, delivering what customers—and users—want via the channel, device, and timing they want.

Digital transformation disrupts the status quo by promoting the customer as the fulcrum of business, then redefining business models, processes, and workflows to flex with and address dynamic customer conversations, needs, and wants. When successful, everyone wins—the customers, users, leaders, partners, stakeholders and even the industry.

Three Tipping Points to Pivot Disruption

As rewarding as the latent potential is when found through disruption, there is an inevitable tipping point—actually three of them—to convert that disruption into opportunity.

The first tipping point is flexibility. When a company is flexible and open to new possibilities, adapts to circumstances and events, and is ready to 'twist' existing resources into a new shape, there is resilience. Resilience ensures that an organization bends and flows with change, malleable through the tough times, and available to grow in new ways.

The second tipping point is technology, given our current digital economy. Technology must be your organization's friend that bridges every aspect, team, and individual to generate and deliver value through automation, collaboration, and real-time data for insightful decision-making. Technology connects people, teams, data, operations, backend and frontend systems… it's the essential silver thread in any enterprise today. It's important to evaluate technological needs, gaps, and potential to facilitate peak performance and new opportunities.

Note: technology will NOT replace human connection; instead, it facilitates it so real-time conversations are more focused and productive.

The third tipping point is marketing. Marketing is the pulse that monitors the beating heart of the organization, then shares what is happening. Where there is disruption, there is a need to communicate clearly. It becomes important to use media channels, marketing materials, and messaging that cuts through the noise and distills the chaos into greater distinction and, ultimately, brand loyalty.

During times of economic disruption, the purpose of marketing becomes focused on communication vs. revenue extraction. Marketing needs to focus on solving and serving, educating, learning about audience issues and concerns, listening to audience(s) and even expanding that audience through targeted, valuable content. At that time, marketing should be a part of, or at least privy to, how the company's path is shaping.

Even during disruption, business still occurs—just with different customer priorities, preferences, and buying patterns. Marketing communicates how a company leads in the 'new normal', sharing stories that illustrate the hard work your company does to support customers, and invites the audience to participate in new conversations.

Bonus: A fourth tipping point in thriving through disruption is empathy. People do the best they can with what they have and know in any given moment. Extend empathy and understanding to let people know you understand and, if you don't, just be there with them through disruption. Disruption surfaces—and amplifies—who we are… and we need each other, especially through tough times. Empathy ensures we retain our humanity through the chaos of disruption.

Altogether, disruption—both unexpected and intentional—can surface new opportunities. Disruption can, when embraced and with strategy applied, create surprising strength through the growth that occurs as a result. Marketers can also use the momentum created through disruption and innovation to craft campaign frameworks to build buzz and harness buy-in from all audiences for new levels of relationship and service.

Three Opportunities for Marketers

While there are exponential opportunities for marketers to leverage in today's digital economy, here are the top three disruptions that are creating windows for potential wins enterprises can take advantage of now with the right strategies and systems.

1. The Internet of Things

The Internet of Things (IoT) connects the world through technology. Your smartwatch can program your home thermostat, your car can start without you, your home security service can answer when someone comes to your front door. Similarly, business technologies—cloud technologies, machine learning, real-time marketing campaigns, customer touch points—connect data that can be analyzed and used to better serve customers today as well as forecast and prepare for the future.

2. Competitive Value

The way to provide unique competitive value to your customers is to deeply understand your ideal customer's wants and needs, develop a solution that has nuanced elements, and market it quickly, effectively and with relevance to the right customers. It's not about what any other company is doing—only about the value you see your customers want and need. Differentiation is in the details.

When your company demonstrates on-going innovation based on caring for your audience(s), then follows through with efficiency, quality, and expertise, your company's value will be obvious.

3. Personalized B2B Marketing

Every transaction that happens in business is based on human relationships, which can be strategically cultivated through content in context for personalized marketing. Personalized marketing at scale means providing practical, relevant, targeted information that meets the questions and needs of your ideal persona(s). The more engaged your future customer becomes through your edu-marketing, or educational marketing, the more trust grows and the more likely there is to be interest in your company's solutions.

The magic key to unlocking this journey is to personalize what your buyer experiences based on their interests, preferences, and behaviors to pull them through and further into your business ecosystem. This information is discoverable through harvesting their data within your ecosystem.

Great content isn't enough; instead, customers want the great content in the right context. This is not about mass 'fishing' to touch as many people as possible; instead, this is about tailoring information to individuals or groups of people who fit your ideal persona profile. While brand image attracts attention, it's about focusing on a substantive, quality customer (and user) experience to nurture the relationship.

Note: targeting a persona to provide content in context does not mean presenting an entirely different company to each customer; instead, it's about highlighting relevant solutions and offers that match individual interests.

Given that business is now conducted on the go during the 'in-between' moments of a buyer's day, the window of connection with that future customer can be fleeting. It's important that companies meet buyers where they are in the moment, in their buying journey, in their connection with the brand overall. This means using real-time integrated data to provide meaningful information that matches the buyer's needs and interests at that time because, typically, the company that provides the most current information and solutions wins the business.

Map the customer journey with your brand—what information draws future customers in, where they see it in their world, what platform they use to find it and how they complete the exchange—to plan your user digital experience. More knowledgeable consumers mean companies have to work harder than ever to find and keep their customers… and nothing works better than tailoring real-time, relevant, and authentic conversations to make that happen. Know where and when the journey should lead and make sure your digital properties are optimized for mobile to minimize lost conversions.

Let's consider specific disruptions that are affecting customer experiences today.

Six Disruptions Affecting CX

Brands today must be agile and adapt their customer experience to both audience expectations and the pace of collective change to remain competitive. It used to be enough to offer the right products in the right place at the right time; today it's also about meeting your customer's perceptions of their relationship with your company's brand. Their perceptions are formed based on their unique touch-points at all times of the day, from wherever they are and via the device of their choice. How your company values your customers is made evident through how your experiences are connected, person-alized, and delivered.

It's important to know that customers hold as a standard for all brands their last best experience. That is, your company's brand is being measured against your customer's experience with Uber, Ama-zon, Walmart, Macy's, Lowe's, and many other household names. That said, here are six key disruptions shaping customer experience in today's business landscape.

1. The Increased Pace of Change

Between advances in technology, a 24/7 digital economy, and access through the IoT, what was news yesterday is old news today. Compa-nies need to keep up with, or even set, the pace of change with their customers. That means staying tuned in to understand what is useful, meaningful, and desirable to your ideal audience(s).

2. Customer Data and Privacy

Data collection happens explicitly and implicitly. Explicit collection requires active participation by the customer, such as in web surveys. Implicit collection comes without the customer's express knowledge, such as through search habits. Regardless of which method, brands are collecting abundant customer data—more than ever before in his-tory, creating a need to ensure customer data is protected and private. Use both collection techniques appropriately by being clear and trans-parent about what you are doing and how you are using the informa-tion to build trust. Then translate the information into actionable insights. Where that interpretation is too complicated or does not yield value, that data could go unused.

In addition to being able to explore and manipulate data for analysis, companies must be aware of legislative regulations governing customer data privacy. There are compliance requirements that must be upheld throughout the data lifecycle for each customer.

3. Artificial Intelligence (AI) And Machine Learning (ML)

Technology that learns from historical results to then shape the customer experience is now the norm and part of what customers expect for their frictionless experience with a brand. The online menu of your favorite restaurant will likely present your favorite selections, while your computer predicts your music choices based on your patterns and preferences, and your GPS will point the way home until you enter a different destination. This accumulated knowledge allows marketers to provide hyper-personalization of content and highly responsive service to any questions or concerns.

4. Voice Recognition and Intelligent Bots

From a marketing perspective in delivering a quality customer experience, using intelligent 'bots' to interact with buyers and customers can save time and resources while being efficient, helpful and personalized in self-service scenarios. For example, future homeowners can pre-qualify for a mortgage through a chatbot, voice prompts can direct a caller to the right resources, and customer service calls decrease as only the most complex situations are referred for human intervention.

5. Video

Customers are conditioned to watch video via television and movies. With recent events, customers are becoming accustomed to video and virtual reality product demos, online education, and meeting via video chat. That means video is now a pillar of digital marketing.

Additionally, Google uses video view time to determine the relevance of a website to determine whether to direct search traffic (or not); the longer the video watch time, the greater the relevance (presumably), which affects the amount of organic traffic directed to a company's website.

6. The Seamless Omnichannel Experience

Customers now expect a unified experience with brands, meaning they don't want to endure multiple systems and apps to do what they want to do. Regardless of the access point, device used, or channel—website, social media, chat, call center, etc., customers want continuous and contiguous efficiency. Seamless customer experience across all channels, applying intelligence to the relationship journey with your brand, and integrating systems to share relevant brand presence at all stages of the customer lifecycle all represent a way to outperform your competitors.

While these disruptions may be daunting, they represent a path to generating new possibilities and opportunities. Let's move on to how marketers can use these disruptors to tailor their customer experience(s).

Marketing Must Tailor CX

Whether it is flight times to book a trip, the best hotel for a destination or an item related to previous purchases, the modern customer demands proper context above all else. They don't want to start searches from the beginning over and over again. They want faster browsing to get to what they want. Ads, promotions, and suggestions must be relevant, timely, and practical. Irrelevant ads not only fail to interest customers but can also actively damage brand credibility for the advertiser in the eyes of that customer.

Providing the right digital experience to potential customers requires vigilance and thoughtful planning but the methods are no mystery. Essentially, you need to get personal to build authentic relationships. To do that means leveraging technology, meaning the entire ecosystem must become frictionless, and experiences must be thoughtfully designed.

The old way of conducting business—where profit was the starting point—has given way to the customer being the starting point of all enterprise. Marketers need to understand the customer's mindset, points of resolution in buying decisions, and unmet needs to highlight the value of your offerings. Systems, especially when designed strategically, can facilitate customer-centricity throughout the organization on multiple levels.

Companies may postpone personalizing customer experiences, managing the touch points, upshifting sales into being digitally enabled. But that is the new norm for customers. They expect instant access to their service requests, statements and invoices, estimates, transactions, information, and more. Customers don't want to have to wait to have a conversation—for either sales or service—unless there's just no way to proceed without it.

In short, successful enterprises today focus on the people—including customers—first with technology, workflows and business systems supporting that focus—and the natural result is profit.

The Organizational Hierarchy of Needs

There is a theory in psychology that you may already know—Maslow's Hierarchy of Needs. It looks like a pyramid, with the more 'base' needs at the bottom, meaning that these needs are essential to human life. Going up the pyramid levels, the psychological needs become more community-oriented and, finally, focused on self-actualization. Starting from the bottom, the levels of the pyramid include:

physiological, safety, love and belonging, esteem and self-actualiza-tion. The theory states that the needs at the bottom of the pyramid must be met before the ones on higher levels; that is, once food, shelter, and water are handled, then a person can begin to think about their place in a community.

Organizations can also apply this theory to business structure and operations. Consider the below graphic showing Maslow's Hierarchy in a business entity context. The left side shows the psychological needs; when the needs of each level are met, financial stability natu-rally increases– think of it as a by-product of taking the right action in the right order.

ORGANIZATIONAL HIERARCHY OF NEEDS

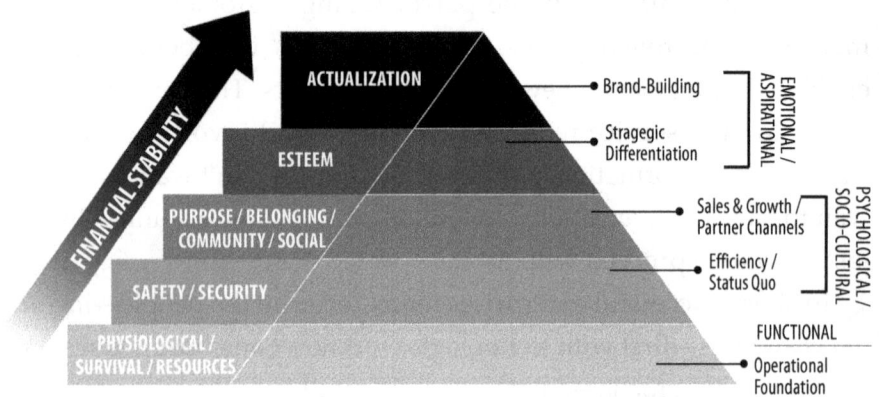

The right side of the graphic indicates that the first level is all about basic functionality—the physiology, the body, of the organization. This means being able to survive as an entity by being able to conduct trans-actions, have cash flow, hire the right people, know the core capabili-ties, have a workplace / structure, and address basic business capabilities.

Once basic functionality has been established, the next two levels account for efficiency, connection with others, corporate culture, and social aspects of the company (such as online presence, memberships, associations, partnerships, etc.).

The second level, Safety and Security, is about efficiency and creating a status quo. The focus is on developing structure, like predictable revenue and profitability, gaining a foothold in the market, putting processes in place, upgrading employee benefits, and getting a rhythm for business operations.

The third level emphasizes belonging-ness in terms of community and relationship needs. This is where the focus is on expanding sales, establishing partnerships, deepening customer relationships, engaging employees, fostering cross-selling and team building and cross-team projects, cultivating significance in the market, establishing vendor relationships, and anything related to enhancing community.

The final two levels—fourth and fifth—focus on aspirational growth and emotional intelligence. This is where the organization clarifies their differentiation through recognition and considers the greater good.

The fourth level distills marketing differentiation strategically on a number of levels, from increasing employee benefits, to upgrading customer experiences, to expanding IT system capabilities, to seeking awards and titles within their industry.

The highest (fifth) level means the organization has reached a level of comfortable, predictable success and so focuses on self-actualization in the bigger picture. Actions to expect here include gifting results at no cost, offering service-based initiatives and philanthropy, becoming a thought leader for additional authority and expanded opportunities, and participating in activities of corporate social responsibility.

Following is what the Hierarchy looks like filled in with these activities.

ORGANIZATIONAL HIERARCHY OF NEEDS

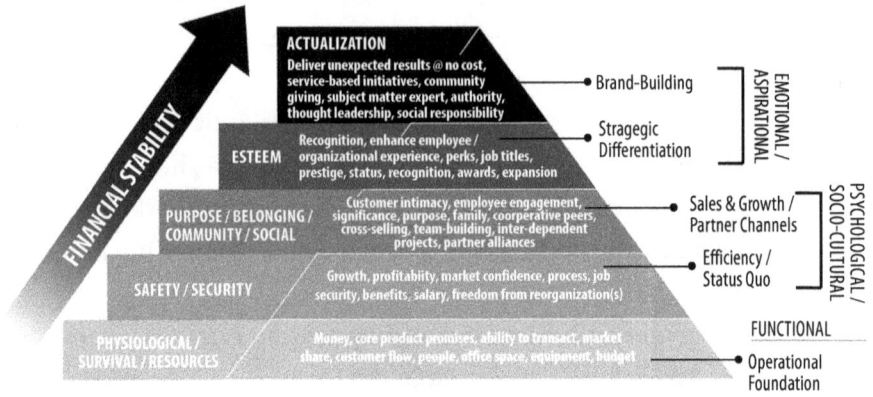

While this gives you a framework to consider how these stages of growth match where your organization is, there is another 'spin' on this Hierarchy—what it looks like from the customer's perspective.

The Customer's Point of View

The following graphic shows your company's Hierarchy from the customer point of view.

On the left side, you see the familiar names of each level. The interior levels show what your customers need and expect from your brand. The right side shows what your organization needs to provide to sustain customer relationships and, ultimately, cultivate mutual loyalty.

The bottom two levels, as in the initial explanation of the Hierarchy, are about basic functionality and establishing a sense of security. These two levels combine to deliver a frictionless experience to both customers and staff.

The first level requires that your customers' basic needs be met in terms of your solution—delivery of their purchase, communication about what to expect and how to implement, and access to support if

THE LOYALTY HIERARCHY | CUSTOMER POV

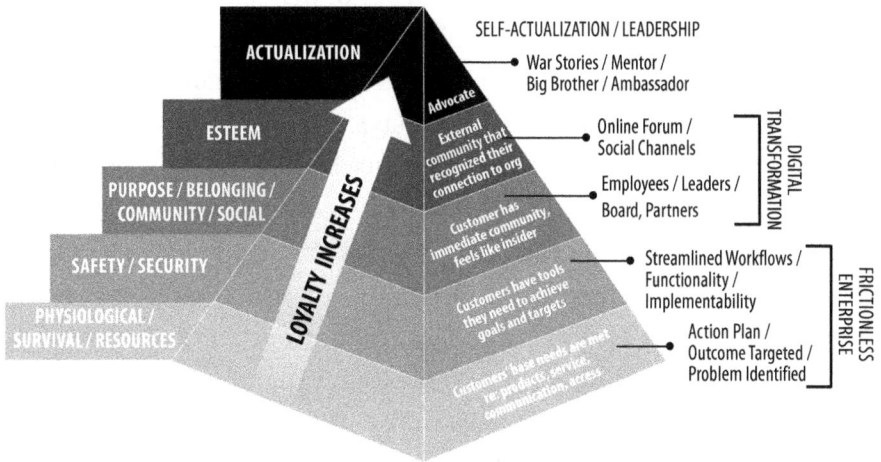

ACTUALIZATION

SELF-ACTUALIZATION / LEADERSHIP
War Stories / Mentor /
Big Brother / Ambassador

ESTEEM

Advocate

External community that recognized their connection to org

Online Forum /
Social Channels

Employees / Leaders /
Board, Partners

DIGITAL TRANSFORMATION

PURPOSE / BELONGING /
COMMUNITY / SOCIAL

Customer has immediate community, feels like insider

SAFETY / SECURITY

Customers have tools they need to achieve goals and targets

Streamlined Workflows /
Functionality /
Implementability

PHYSIOLOGICAL /
SURVIVAL / RESOURCES

Customers' base needs are met re: products, service, communication, access

Action Plan /
Outcome Targeted /
Problem Identified

FRICTIONLESS ENTERPRISE

LOYALTY INCREASES

they need it. This is the core premise—you had this problem, our company has this solution that you purchased, here is how you use it to get the expected outcome.

The second level of the pyramid indicates customers need security through having the tools promised to achieve the expected results. To do so, your organization should provide streamlined implementation guidelines, functionality, and workflows for their solution.

The third level of the pyramid shows that customers need to feel they are an insider with the organization, that they are part of a community, with access to important people and a way to express their thoughts directly.

The fourth level of the pyramid is about your company's community—both internal and external—recognizing your customer's relationship with the organization. This social status occurs through awards, social media, online forums, conferences and events, and personal networking opportunities.

The combined the third and fourth levels represent the benefits of digital transformation in that your organization has to be organized and robust enough to deliver these types of deliverables.

The highest level of the pyramid, the fifth level, enables your customer to become a company ambassador. As they share their success, naturally your company is a part of that story and it becomes inviting to others to have a similar transformation. To support these outcomes, your organization needs to give customers the language with which to communicate their success story—case studies, video interviews, newsletter spotlights, conference speaking opportunities. In doing this, your organization demonstrates leadership through that customer's success story. Naturally, your organization expands its visibility and reach in the market. This also lends itself to positioning thought leadership content in context of customer successes.

The Significance of the Hierarchy of Needs

While it may not be obvious, there are several reasons why understanding this Hierarchy of Needs can be helpful to your organization.

1. Until lower needs have been met, organizations (and their initiatives) cannot grow financial stability by moving into higher levels. This single insight can help companies understand why expected growth has not yet happened.

2. Transformation is destabilizing to people, processes, and profit centers. When that happens, people may not be able to adapt, which creates (consciously or subconsciously) resistance to change. By understanding the Hierarchy, you can predict and, ideally, neutralize the challenges change inherently brings.

3. When change out-paces peoples' ability to adapt to it, change can slow, stall, or even become blocked. When digital transformation does not, or cannot, occur, your competitors

can out-innovate your solution and/or marketplace position. By supporting the psychological needs of your staff and leaders, your company optimizes the transformation adjustment, which supports having a competitive edge in the market.

4. By progressing through the first four levels, an organization will reach the fifth level of self-actualization. In that case, the organization needs to fulfill that mandate and operate at that level or risk losing ground. It's similar to a master artist using a paint by numbers kit... it doesn't make sense to waste the talent, the resources, they have earned the right to express.

5. The higher the level at which an organization finds itself, the greater the financial stability. That's because the ecosystem has been built, reinforced, and expanded to accommodate reaching ever-higher levels.

The point of Maslow's Hierarchy that's relevant to organizations is that there is a growth journey for companies. Organizations move through these hierarchical levels at various stages of lifecycle, from individual employees to the team to the whole company. Know where your organization is to support your customers, employees, partners, and goals properly. With that knowledge, it is simpler to identify and pursue new potential opportunities and revenue sources.

Woke Leadership

Nobody knows what digital transformation will look like in every company. In fact, it's impossible to say because every company has its unique needs, circumstances, and resources. However, since my focus is on actualizing potential, aka transformation, I am including some of what I know about the process of digital transformation in case it might be helpful to you and your organization.

Making the Case for Digital Transformation

There are three major steps to making the case for digital transformation for next-gen customer (and user) experience: vision the possibilities, assess the now, and create the plan for priorities, actions, and investments.

Organizations allot resources to support reaching business targets. Accordingly, new initiatives need to project at least a break-even return or greater. It has to make sense on a business level to allocate needed resources to a digital transformation initiative.

As a champion for digital transformation, your goal is to present the case for growth with a tangible vision and solid Return on Investment (ROI). You want to make sure there's long-term and short-term benefits as well as key performance indicators (KPIs) in there. Regardless of your position within the organization, you want to ask for help from company leaders and managers to frame the transformation in terms of goals and objectives, and get buy-in from colleagues as well.

Accordingly, the more imminent the benefits of the growth initiative in producing positive results, the more likely funds will be allocated toward that initiative. So if the innovation will produce results significant enough, it might be possible to secure additional funding, such as through investors or other sources. However, that means the growth initiative must be described in terms of business benefits.

Understanding how growth investments in the past have been received by and impacted your company can be a helpful indicator of what's going to happen with current growth proposals. All companies founded by an entrepreneur or a group of entrepreneurs who understand risk balance and trying something new have been through the growth analysis experience, but most managers have not. Managers are different from entrepreneurs.

Either way, you have to "sell" the growth. That can be especially challenging if the growth idea initiates bottom-up, meaning frontline staff see the opportunity and need to promote it up the corporate ladder. Conversely, if frontline staff doesn't buy into the growth opportunity, it's difficult to get adoption and, often, they have the most impact in implementing the change(s). You can see that it's important to share the growth process and projections throughout your entire organization.

The good news is that, even if not all managers are naturally inclined to break the status quo and grow, they're usually aligned on initiatives that provide positive growth for the business. And when growth is an outcome, it's something that's going to get supportive attention.

You can also look at what's going to happen if you don't grow. There is an opportunity cost in terms of the competition taking the lead, becoming obsolete when you're not looking and missing opportunities. Is the cost of taking on growth less than the cost of not pursuing it?

That is a deceptively simple question, especially when you factor in what could happen if your competitor invested in that growth and your company did not. One way to test that is to wait and see what happens in the market. It's risky, because your competitors could become market leaders, but it's a passive test that will yield insights.

The growth initiative has to have a way to transition the work needed to support it in a fast track kind of way or it might be not so viable by the time people get to it. So, once you put a growth initiative in play, you might find unexpected challenges, opportunities, environmental issues, feedback from the market, or whatever other things might come up that need to be accommodated. So just know that disruption of the status quo is a byproduct of growth. Current workflows and operations may need to shift to accommodate this new project or initiative, which can meet resistance when people are uncomfortable with change. So you have to be prepared to help your colleagues understand the benefits—paint the potential wins, the quick wins, the overall results in a powerful, vibrant, and meaningful way. And when this is all done well, you are going to potentially have significant change throughout the organization as that growth project becomes assimilated and is the "new normal."

Leadership Roles and Responsibilities

Three roles are principally charged with leading digital transformation:

1. The Chief Executive Officer (CEO), who sets the mandate for it,

2. The Chief Marketing Officer (CMO), who handles the strategy for supporting your customer-centric lifecycle, and

3. The Chief Information Officer (CIO), who handles the execution of technology.

Disruption will occur from all three vantage points and all three will need to make new investments to achieve a positive outcome. What got you to your current state will not get you to your desired state. Digital transformation is the result of the commitment and investments organizations make to remain competitive, relevant, and viable.

CEO

The CEO does three things:

1. Sees the future,

2. Reports on what they see and handle crises,

3. Acknowledges and thanks staff and leadership for day-to-day business operations.

When seeing the future, digital transformation becomes a significant priority because it includes the elements that will ensure an organization remains competitive in the market—streamlined operations, value-laden connections, deepening relationships, customer-centric operations, etc. The woke CEO's role is to issue the mandate for digital transformation, then provide support as needed to those who help make it happen.

CIO

The CIO's role has evolved as a result of business leaders' expectations that technology is the conduit to achieving business transformation. At first, it was enough that CIOs kept mainframe technology systems going and stable. Then it became about client/server technology to create competitive advantage through leverage. These two phases were deliberate, emphasizing low personnel costs, and sequential, forward-only development initiatives.

Now CIOs must be more strategic, and focus is on inter-dependencies between cloud computing, mobile computing, big data, social media, analytics, and emerging technologies. Agility is needed to take advantage of fast-moving opportunities using technology's speed, global availability, and cost-effectiveness. Innovation is a key strategy to develop and refine initiatives to meet business needs (both current and emerging). Customer experience and collaboration are focal points to maximize business value. Project management is now iterative where failing forward faster is the mantra for success.

Altogether, digital transformation will result in upgraded workflows, data, and performance. Silos can no longer exist, whether operational, cultural, or technical. Data holds the master key to new opportunities, identifying trends, and projecting market shifts. The woke CIO combines the technology, systems, data, trends, insights, and projections that underscore and propel digital transformation. Their responsibility is much more than keeping the lights on... it's about next-level competitive advantage and long-term sustainability for their organization.

CMO

Marketing today means brands need an always-on, omni-channel, on-demand presence. As previously shared, the traditional marketing funnel has been replaced by a paddlewheel powered by customer needs, wants, and expectations. Customers expect their needs, wants and problems to be anticipated, with the solutions accessible where they are already looking, delivered with strategic and personalized experiences via invisible technology.

CMOs are charged with shepherding the customer lifecycle from attraction through advocacy; to do so means shaking and breaking the status quo with fresh perspectives and new campaigns on the go based on real-time business intelligence. Already unpopular as a result,

CMOs often discover 'mushroom cloud' issues lurking under the surface that must be addressed for the sake of cohesive customer experience, market positioning, customer expectations and more to deliver a unified customer journey. Accordingly, the CMO must lead developing the customer experience while simultaneously aligning the organization's capability to deliver it in a way that others can understand and support.

Business today requires using real-time analytics to not only meet customers where they are but to be where customers will be, along with automating routine tasks, leveraging software intelligence, and offering hyper-connectivity based on customer needs and expectations. CMOs therefore need to know intimately the customer and their journey to design experiences that are relevant, practical, and timely. They also need to understand the organization's culture to normalize the shifts required to become increasingly customer-centric.

CMO and CIO Alignment

CMOs are masters of alignment in terms of making connections between people, issues, and solutions, empowering both clarity and action, persuading buy-in, and uniting disparate parts and pieces. These are pivotal skills when it comes to leading a digital transformation initiative. So is partnering with the CIO so they can be effective in working with systems, data, and workflows to deliver meaningful customer experiences.

The CIOs mandate is to care for all culture- and customer-facing systems—customer data, business intelligence, machine learning systems, service delivery and more. Woke CMOs need to profoundly understand the customer. The CIO needs to connect all internal systems to build a unified, dynamic profile of the customer(s) so you as the CMO have a full-spectrum picture of the buying journey. The CIO can show you your customers' journey, preferences, needs, interests, behaviors, touchpoints, timeline, requests for more information... all of it.

The role of the woke CMO is to then translate that information into a viable profile to deliver a strategically crafted experience that meets the customer wherever they are in their brand experience at any time and on any device. There is no longer a separation between attracting a customer and a salesperson taking over that relationship; instead, each customer's unique experience is seamless and supported at the right time by the right information and right employee function.

Technology is no longer an optional consideration for marketing activities; instead, technology is now the essential launchpad and integrator of company-wide marketing initiatives, decision-making and customer-centric operations. Technology can unify the customer journey, optimize functions, reveal trends for decision-making; at the same time, the CMO must make the most of what technology cannot do—empower employees to build authentic, trusted relationships.

By combining the respective expertise, knowledge, and skills sets required of woke leadership, cultural alignment within the organization naturally progresses. The woke CMO knows digital marketing has upshifted, actualizing through a digital transformation process; the woke CIO applies their technical expertise, systems knowledge, and experience toward supporting the organization's digital transformation mandate.

Organizational Culture

Organizational culture is the cumulative result of leadership in action and employee contributions; the Evolved CMO recognizes that each individual plays a role in serving customers, regardless of specific job duties. Digital transformation can shake employee confidence in terms of their future relevance, job security, and daily activities going forward, even when employees understand the outcome will be delivering greater value for more satisfied customers. CMOs can reduce resistance by recognizing the importance of each employee's contribution by sharing outside-in thinking.

That is, employees may think if they 'just do this thing' (aka, inside-out thinking—my task starts and ends here), they will have done their job. However, digital transformation requires an outside-in mindset where the job starts with customers who have names and problems employees can solve when they 'do this thing' faster and more efficiently. CMOs are uniquely positioned to convey the vision around helping employees design and deliver a stellar customer experience because they can engage customers, share successes, and ensure employees are included to 'own' their part in creating customer happiness and organizational results.

The One Key Question

The woke CMO needs to lead digital transformation through (communicating) vision, sharing knowledge, being a shock absorber for change, and strategic resource allocation while—simultaneously—find, develop, and live on the growing edge of organizational, market, or industry innovation. It takes courage to go beyond the comfort zones (the status quo) where others have never been… there is no one-size-fits-all approach to digital transformation. The woke CMO's ability to 'dance' with circumstances as they present will promote digital transformation progress and victory throughout the organization.

There is no clear sign for every organization that it is time to undergo digital transformation. However, there is one question that can guide and orient a woke CMO's focus in leading digital transformation.

How can every digital touchpoint and every employee interaction engage each customer as a unique person to cultivate 1:1 conversation and build relationship(s)?

The answers will inform how digital transformation proceeds in your organization. It is likely nothing—no process, no workflow, no campaign, no role—will remain untouched because it includes everything from data enablement to customer profiling to journey mapping to cross-team collaboration to training on systems and software. Enterprise-wide digital transformation is facilitated by a high-level holistic vision and perspective tempered by current circumstances and resources, supported by technology systems, and delivered through employees and technology at every level. Shaking the status quo will surface challenges… AND new opportunities.

Embarking on a digital transformation journey drives company leadership to unite and prepare for the future while delivering customer value today. Being a woke CMO means doing it all seamlessly in today's Experience Economy. Even more, by virtue of strategizing and coordinating contiguous results along the entire value chain, a woke CMO understands the true measure of success for their organization—being visibly invisible. That is, the transformational changes seem natural and obvious, yet without effort and dramatic confrontation between the current and the new.

Counter to what you might think, many leaders lack the cross-functional skills needed for next-level strategic planning. Where there is a gap in leadership skills, digital transformation can stall or even stop. In this case, it could be advantageous to hire or consult with professionals who have the skills to develop strategies, frameworks, and teams to achieve your transformation targets. Additionally, be sure to look for internal champions who can support the process as well.

Conditions will never be perfect to begin a digital transformation process. Every passing week means a week when your competitors or market are in their own transformation processes, which means you cannot afford to not know about digital transformation. Even so, when considering best practices for digital transformation, your company's process will not look like any other company's process. There is no one-size-fits-all option because each organization has a unique history and vision. The single most effective way to orchestrate digital transformation in your company is to use your brand and customers experiences as a gauge for what's possible, then work to achieve it.

B2B Marketing in the Digital Experience Economy

Consumers are sophisticated, knowledgeable, and empowered; ultimately, they determine a company's long-term destiny. Why? Because their perceptions—of value, of trust, of efficiency, of delight—determine their buying decisions and length of relationship with a company. Profit is simply a by-product of ensuring customers gain value at every stage of their experience. The key to shaping perceptions, both with the market and with buyers and customers, happens through marketing.

Traditional marketing has evolved—what worked 'then' does not work 'now' (or at least not the same way). Individual touchpoints need to be honed into a larger experience in context that can be personalized to individual buyers and customers. It's not enough to digitize content and operations; it's now vital to have a strategy in place to guide building relationships and positive brand experiences.

Traditionally, marketers used a funnel approach which visually looks like an ice cream cone, where buyers are attracted into the funnel at the top and move down through stages into a purchase decision. The stages of the buying journey in this model include: Attract, Convert, Delight, Advocate.

In the B2B buying journey, in the largest sense, the same stages must be considered and enabled; however, the potential customer is typically more than one person on behalf of a company, their interest level is relative to their pain points and understanding of possible solutions, and they have their own responsibilities (such as validation and consensus-building) within those four stages. Therefore, each customer persona has different triggers for their buying decisions throughout their journey with a brand.

Today's B2B customer is typically more than one person as decisions are made by committee(s). The buying decision is comprised of cumulative research that fulfills the roles needed for the organization vs. a linear sequence of progression through a buying journey. According to analyst firm Gartner, these six roles are: problem identification, solution exploration, requirements building, supplier selection, validation, and consensus creation.

These six roles are met through research, content consumption, and self-service as much as possible. This is consistent with buyer behavior in general—just think about what you do when considering a major purchase. Most people will now go online, read whatever they can find at various touchpoints (in brand or not), take a look at reviews and social proof, assess the brand's online presence and credibility, and form a foundation for educated options that warrant further conversation.

The key to resolving milestone questions and objections for buyers to achieve a purchase decision is ensuring your brand has differentiation that translates into intentional, memorable experiences that build trust, credibility, and relationship.

Correspondingly, the B2B marketer needs both strategy and action steps designed to resolve those questions and objections to help the buyer move through their purchase journey. Following are quick definitions of relevant terms for this process because, too often, marketers need to explain them to colleagues and don't know how to do it.

Demand gen, or 'top of funnel' strategy in traditional terms, attracts attention, clarifies the problems buyers are experiencing, and generates awareness of a brand and its offerings. Demand gen marketing, when done well, helps B2B buyers with problem identification, solution exploration, and requirements building. Tactics that work well for demand gen include: content marketing, video marketing, display ads, social media marketing, and search engine optimization (SEO).

Lead gen takes over the process, which is the middle of the funnel in traditional terms, to convert buyers into taking action. There is an exchange of information from the organization with contact information and specific solutions needs or requirements from the potential buyer. Lead gen helps buyers with supplier selection, solution validation, and consensus creation with colleagues about a particular solution.

Retention and advocacy comprise the loyalty loop, or what was traditionally the bottom of the funnel, where customers cycle back up to the top of the funnel by identifying new problems and opportunities to upgrade or enhance their challenges by purchasing next-level solutions.

By the way, brand gen (generation) is the overarching visibility a particular brand has in a market. Brand gen is what household names are doing with tv commercials; the idea behind brand gen is to create a known presence in a market. Brand gen is different from demand gen (creating interest in offers) and/or lead gen (converting interest into selling conversations). Demand generation is undertaking activities with the goal of attracting potential customers by creating interest in your offers. Lead generation is converting that interest into specific contact information for the sales team or pipeline for follow through to have selling conversations.

One approach for marketers to use in a customer-centric culture is '360-Degree Digital Marketing.' This methodology places the buyer at the center of ten significant B2B marketing strategies as follows:

1. A great website

2. Social media marketing

3. Video marketing

4. Content marketing

5. Search engine optimization (SEO)

6. Pay-per-click advertising (PPC)

7. Event marketing (including virtual)

8. Partners and affiliates

9. Retargeting

10. Marketing automation (including email marketing)

Obviously, the above is a short list of attributes and considerations as each could be its own book, and each could apply to multiple stages of the buying journey. The idea is, no matter the strategy, it always goes back to the marketer to consider and enhance the potential buyer's experience and brand value.

Buyer Enablement Through Targeted Content

Content marketing is an all-encompassing term that includes blogs, news articles, social media, email workflows, videos, press releases, FAQs, newsletters, e-books, white papers, special reports, case studies, infographics, datasheets, and more. In the absence of content, marketing lacks substance and the ability to provide value through narrative.

Given the trend for buyers to do as much self-service research before talking to a salesperson, B2B marketers need to think "buyer enablement" for content, meaning content that supports the completion of critical buying tasks.

To build buyer enablement content, marketing leaders need to understand the points of resolution and tasks that buyers need to accomplish and experience in their buying journey, provide information that addresses these tasks, and then provide access to this information through the buyers' preferred channels. Content needs to be positioned where buyers are already looking to be most easily consumed.

When it comes to buyer enablement, think about the problem the content is solving and make sure it addresses that part of the buying journey. For example, when it comes to demand gen, blogs and webinars are great. For lead gen, you're solving for a different problem: conversion.

For lead gen, it's important to help buyers through the tasks of supplier selection, solution validation, and consensus creation. Content pieces suited for lead gen include case studies, testimonials, reviews, press releases, blurbs about awards and partnerships, white papers, information about the company's culture, history, and core values, and anything that would build credibility and authority in short, digestible form.

When it comes to supporting customer retention, content marketing is just as vital as it is during the buying journey because it is far more profitable to sell to an existing customer than to a new one. Satisfied customers will likely begin a new buying journey with your company when they have awareness of a new need, product, solution, upgrade and/or addition to what they already have with you.

The top five types of content marketing that are ideal for customer retention and repeat business include blogs, ebooks and whitepapers, social media, videos, and webinars. Email marketing is an excellent way to deliver all of this content, except social media, to remain top-of-mind with your current customers.

Email marketing helps your customers learn about new offers, relevant insights, potential deals from your company. Email marketing can also include (and is not limited to) the following types of formats and topics for communication and to build relationships.

- Monthly newsletters
- Blog newsletters
- Webinar invitations and notifications
- New service offering notifications
- Thank you and culture-building emails
- New ebook or resource announcements
- Staff introduction emails

Essentially, you want to empower your customers by educating them with substantive information and insight. Additionally, reading your brand messaging helps build their vocabulary to be able to talk about your services when sharing about their business successes.

Just as importantly, remember to minimize talking about the company—the focus of content needs to be about the buyer and/or customer. Also, do not emphasize solution features; do focus on benefits to the buyer. Make sure content is written by someone with experience or expertise to avoid 'fluff' content. And keep content concise at about, or less than, 2,000 words or three to five minutes in video.

The Big Four: Vision, Mission, Values, Purpose

Vision, mission, values, and purpose are critical elements of an organization's brand identity, strategic planning process, and decision-making criteria. And yet, I am surprised by the companies who have never taken the time, either initially or afterward, to go through the exercise of articulating the 'Big Four.' Following is a breakdown of each term as well as ideas on how you can create your own statements for each.

Vision describes how the future will look when the Mission is achieved. Vision defines what the organization wants to become and achieve; it is usually bigger than the organization can achieve in a life-time to keep pulling the enterprise toward it. A vision statement should clearly communicate the overall goals of the company and serve as a strategic direction of what is expected to be experienced in the future.

Vision is a primary motivator of human action, clarifying purpose, giving direction, and empowering people to perform beyond their resources. The right Vision is energizing in that it can call in the resources, skills, and talents to make it happen. It should answer the question: what is the final outcome of the work of the enterprise?

To create a Vision statement, write it in the present tense as though it has already happened. See the long game while making it credible, inspiring, and attainable. A great Vision gives meaning to daily activities through inspiring commitment and focused energy. Keep it concise because staff and leadership needs to be able to understand and remember it.

Example: The SavvyX vision is that innovative, relevant, and accountable business brands operate with a new norm—designing and delivering delightful, rewarding, and meaningful customer and employee experiences.

Mission answers the 'what' question—what is work we do, for who, and for what benefit? A Mission statement describes how you will deliver on your Purpose, defining your business model, offers, and/or customers. Your Mission statement becomes a competitive differentiator because it is unique to your company. And it is a guiding compass on how to achieve your Vision.

A Mission statement should be simple enough to be recited by memory, no more than one sentence. It should include what your company does, how it does it, and who is served by your company's solutions. Following is a simple formula to help you craft your company's Mission statement.

Our mission is to (verb), (core value/s) (to, for or with) (your key audiences).

Example 1: Our mission is to craft compelling, holistic brand development strategy and messaging for mid-level B2B enterprises ready to grow their audiences through savvier experiences.

Example 2: Our mission is to punch holes in B2B brand comfort zones to facilitate savvy experiences so companies can drive more business, dissolve barriers and be more agile in delivering intentional experiences.

Values are the foundational ethics that guide decision-making, behavior, and action in your company. Values help staff and leadership know what is right (or wrong) and helps determine if the right path has been set to achieve the company's goals.

Your Values act as a powerful choice filter and magnet, attracting people and opportunities that enrich and serve your company.

In identifying your Values, you should select no more than five values that represent the 'soul' of your company; those Values should be part of every aspect of your company. Sample values include such things as: authenticity, ambition, authority, balance, community, competency, client-focused, curious, excellence, fun, growth, happiness, honesty, integrity, innovation, kindness, knowledge, meaningful, optimistic, passionate, respectful, stable, trustworthy, team-oriented, unified, etc.

Example:

- We value time for ourselves and our customers.
- We value freedom in being able to flex, shift and expand with creativity in every moment.
- We value people who want to work and play well together personally and professionally.
- We value full experiences with full-on joy, laughter, and open transparency.

- We value people for who they are outside of their roles and titles.
- We value making a bigger difference through positive outcomes every day.

Purpose is the reason your enterprise exists. It answers the 'why' question (why does X company exist?). Leaders communicate purpose as a means to fulfilling the vision, mission, and values. A Purpose statement points people in the right direction for achievement (organization, team, and personal).

Defining your Purpose requires consideration about the organization's passion points, what inspired founding the company, and what compels action daily. The Purpose statement should be aspirational, challenging, and attainable.

A formula you can use to define your Purpose statement follows.

To (<u>what company X wants to achieve, do or become</u>)
so that (<u>reasons why it is important</u>).

We will do this by (<u>specific behaviors or actions you can use to get there</u>).

Example: Our purpose is to strategize savvy B2B experiences for companies to use so that they can increase their visibility, attract and retain customers, and have greater loyalty in relationships long-term.

We will do this by discovering their current situation and desired outcome(s), strategize new approaches, build experiences to meet customers' dynamic needs, use data to measure momentum, and iterate for continuous improvement.

Brand Archetypes

When the vision, mission, values, and purpose have been identified and articulated, their combination reveals how a brand might show up as an entity, similar to a person with characteristics and qualities. That is called a brand archetype, which is an important yet often overlooked marketing strategy.

Archetypes are universal patterns of behavior that help us understand what motivates an individual. "That guy is such a rebel." From that statement alone, we can make certain assumptions about the character, personality, and motivations of that person. The same holds true for brands because, when known and made intentional, signify a company's mission, brand promise, and culture. For example, Harley Davidson and Apple fit the brand archetype of rebel.

The brand archetype can facilitate the experience of the company and be the foundation of why it attracts certain customers. If you do not know your company's brand archetype, it can mean you don't know who you are or are unclear in your market presence making it hard to attract and engage customers. It makes it challenging to differentiate from your competitors. Without a brand archetype, your company risks being a commodity and having to compete in price wars for business.

If you have different perspectives within your company about your brand archetype, it can (will) cause confusion in the market because staff and leadership are telling different stories. When you stray from your primary archetype, you are not being authentic and risk compromising relationships with your ideal customers.

When your customers do not know who your company is when in a working relationship, the cost could be their loyalty as they seek stability and certainty from competitors.

Here's the good news... your brand archetype gives meaning to your solutions. Your company no longer competes solely on price. Your company becomes differentiated in the market with a clear and relatable position. Your company's overarching brand story is articulated and can be shared consistently. The archetype creates a structural framework by which to convey the meaning of your brand to your ideal audience(s). And, because the meaning of your brand is your company's biggest asset, when people understand instantly what your company stands for, they will form relationships based on emotional and psychological reasons and want to remain loyal over time.

Companies tend to seek the magic silver bullet in marketing—a strategy, plan, technique, angle—that will attract and engage the perfect audience who perceives their solution to be unique and irreplaceable. What is overlooked is that those connections are based on relationships. When a brand is unclear about 'who' it is, people are not going to be interested in the company. So understanding your brand archetype is knowing how to begin a relationship with customers.

An enterprise, while not actually a person, has a distinct character that is embodied in the brand, culture, and language. This character can be hard to acknowledge and bring to life; this is where archetypes can be effectively used to represent a way of thinking that transcends time or age due to referencing classic universal principles. Using an archetype in business for a brand can shift marketing from a 'push' to 'pull' strategy through attraction, from sharing mere messages to conveying values, from transactions to loyal, long-term relationships. Their use in a brand context typically categories them into 12 primary archetypes, symbolizing basic human motivations, meanings, values, and traits.

For example, you know what a brand stands for when a brand archetype is in play… just ask Jack Daniels, the Old Spice Guy, or Orville Redenbacher.

Since successful branding is largely built upon bridging between the offer and how/why people make buying decisions, it is important to understand and negotiate the dynamic tension of four basic drives. The four basic drives are: change, social belonging, order, and individual fulfillment.

Within each of those drives there are three archetypes as follows.

1. Change, which is about freedom, risk, and mastery: Hero, Magician, Jester

2. Social Belonging, which is about community and connection: Lover, Citizen, Caregiver

3. Order, which is about stability and control: Sovereign, Creator, Innocent

4. Individual Fulfillment, which is about independence: Explorer, Sage, Rebel

The **Hero** makes the world better by being the best, and by challenging you to be your best. Nike, US Army
Flavors: Warrior, Athlete, Rescuer, Liberator

Magician brands bring your wildest dreams to life. Disney, Mac Cosmetics, Polaroid
Flavors: Innovator, Alchemist, Engineer, Scientist

The **Jester** lives in the moment and wants to make you smile with light-hearted fun. Old Spice, Progressive, Geico
Flavors: Entertainer, Provocateur, Shapeshifter, Clown

The **Lover** wants you to associate them with the intimate moments in your life. Hallmark, Godiva Chocolate
Flavors: Companion, Hedonist, Matchmaker

The **Citizen** is driven by a sense of integrity, fairness, responsibility and belonging to the community. Budweiser, Wrangler, Folger's Coffee
Flavor: Everyman, Advocate, Servant, Networker

The **Caregiver** nurtures and just wants to be there for you. Johnson & Johnson, Salvation Army
Flavors: Guardian, Samaritan, Healer, Angel

The **Sovereign** is the gatekeeper of luxury and exclusivity, exuding a sense of privilege, royalty, high-quality, and expensive offers. Mercedes-Benz, Rolex
Flavors: Ruler, Judge, Ambassador, Patriarch

The **Creator** strives for perfection and to create a product you can't live without. Lego, Adobe
Flavors: Visionary, Storyteller, Artist, Entrepreneur

The **Innocent** wants happiness and will charm you with nostalgia. Orville Redenbacher, Coca Cola
Flavors: Dreamer, Idealist, Child, Muse

The **Explorer** wants you to leave your comfort zone and break traditions for freedom and adventure. Jeep, REI, NASA
Flavors: Adventurer, Pioneer, Generalist, Seeker

The **Sage** commands respect through wisdom, simplicity, and illustrating brilliance. Harvard University, Mayo Clinic, TED
Flavors: Mentor, Detective, Shaman, Translator, Teacher

The **Rebel** is about fresh perspectives, new outlooks, aspirational change, and awakening, breaking rules, questioning the status quo, and pushing the envelope. Harley Davidson, Jack Daniels, Vans
Flavors: Outlaw, Activist, Gambler, Maverick, Reformer

Archetypes provide a springboard for brand development and form the foundation for common language. Archetypes also influence and increase the company's asset valuation.

The reason brand archetypes work is because they create instant emotional impact which triggers instant affinity through attraction and resonance. Brand archetypes increase trust quickly because their foundation is consistency in behavior and interpretation of meaning over time.

Working with brand archetypes can guide strategy, marketing campaigns, relationships, solution development, marketplace positioning, corporate culture, and more. It can enhance brand reach and impact the bottom-line.

There are a few things you can do to determine your brand archetype. First, think about your brand's personality. At the end of the day, what did your company do, achieve, or create that day? Was the outcome of your work in leading a market, helping a customer realize their dream, or taking care of a customer in crisis? The most satisfying situation is likely the one that is the clue to your company's brand archetype.

You can also review current and previous customer statements and comments about their experience with your company. Pay attention to their language, how they tell their success stories, what led them to working with your company in the first place... these will guide you to seeing your brand's archetype in action.

Research your company with a beginner's mind. That is, go online to see how your company comes up during a search. Consider your content to check what the themes of your narrative messaging are to learn what your audiences are seeing when your company comes to your website. Review case studies and success stories to see if they highlight your best work. Talk to staff and leadership to see how they describe your company. Interview vendors and other stakeholders to learn what they feel is most attractive about your company. All these data points can help you clarify your brand archetype. Note: you may need to lead your team through exercises to help them see and understand your brand archetype.

Once you have identified your brand archetype, you can research and document the language and visuals that most expresses that archetype. You can identify the ideal projects to take on and the buyers who will most resonate with your brand's personality to improve your targeting in marketing. You can create a social media presence and marketing campaigns that speak to that archetype. Even small adjustments can make a surprisingly significant difference.

The Pain and the Power
of Digital Marketing

The marketing team is typically charged with communicating an organization's value, yet sales is often in the field actualizing value with buyers. Value is the glue between messaging and offered solutions. Marketing and sales are on the same continuum as marketing positions for the relationship to develop, and sales personalizes the solution for individual relationships. Both teams need to be in sync around the shared messages of value for a cohesive brand experience.

In terms of expressing a company's value, or brand promise, it should be in every element of marketing, sales, online presence, piece of content, etc. Everything around your brand is an opportunity to showcase the value you offer your customers, which includes your employees, leadership, partners, vendors... every touchpoint is a place to communicate your brand's differentiators and market value.

The digital economy has changed how marketing is done now because people expect seamless, fast, invisible technology to deliver the information they want in the moment and that they can access on the go. In a sales conversation, they want to do preemptive research and options generation on their own. In post-transaction service, people want to do as much as they can on their own to solve problems and meet needs.

As previously stated, business is now as customers drive it. To accommodate this next-level approach, enterprises need to upshift, or transform, their people, processes, and profit centers to be human-centric, deliver perceptive experiences, and be predictively responsive to emerging needs and wants. This is the mandate of digital transformation—to ensure a company's long-term viability and success by sustaining its competitive edge and pacing demands from customers and users.

At first glance, business seems to be about the deal, the transaction, or making the close. The reality is that business is about relationships— between the company and its customers, employees, and industry. These relationships can be facilitated by using technology to automate core functions and identify how to personalize an engagement with a target persona. Technology also streamlines the workflows and processes employees need to support their peak performance and ability to connect with customers and each other.

Digital marketing has transformed business on multiple levels, from digitization to relationship personalization to sales enablement. And, given that people spend a lot of time consuming content in digital channels, the experiences they have with household names set their expectations for the experiences they have with every brand. That means companies are now competing with companies, including in other industries and with much larger budgets, for buyer and customer attention. (Docusign, Uber, Netflix, or any other household brand name with online presence, anyone…?)

Essentially, digital marketing ensures the buyer has the information and ability at the right time and in the right sequence to accomplish their buying tasks and make informed decisions.

Altogether, marketing is now fairly sophisticated. Hyperbole, redundant messages, superlatives… none of that is enough to break through the saturated, intense nature of the market to get attention. Now it's about 'lean' marketing to deliver clear value throughout the customer lifecycle. Value is delivered through a comprehensive range of content, from ebooks to data sheets to gamification, videos, and online tools, through each stage of customer engagement. It's about inspiring, educating, and entertaining to develop a relationship that becomes a paying one.

How does that happen? By understanding the customer buying journey through its complexity for your customers… see what they see, know, and want through data to give them what they need when and where they want it. In terms of monitoring the ROI (return on investment) for marketing tactics, the main ones include those that impact profitability and competitive advantage: cost of customer acquisition, customer lifetime value, website traffic numbers, conversion rates, social media engagement. Then refine your process based on what you learn as you go.

Pain Points for B2B Marketers

There are pain points B2B marketers need to know and, potentially, leverage to be effective in articulating and then promoting brand promise, taking their industry's pulse, educating their teams, and supporting relationship development through the entire marketing and sales continuum.

The first pain point that rubs every technician the wrong way is that buzzwords become real; that is, phrases like 'frictionless enterprise', 'future-proof systems', 'next-level experience', 'invisible technology', and 'digital transformation' become adopted over time to describe much larger concepts. And if the market believes them to be real, they become pivotal conversation points. Having a common language with potential and current customers is how relationships are forged, whether or not that language is technically correct.

Following is a quick snapshot definition of terms.

Frictionless business means systems, processes, and technology work seamlessly without disruption and without being overtly noticeable to customers and users. In the past, friction was generated by a fragmented marketing stack, redundant data capture, disjointed customer profiles, slow feature upgrades, status quo habits, lack of real-time information and more. Today, technology has resolved most of these issues so processes are streamlined and data is unified and enabled.

Altogether, frictionless means having the ability to deliver relevant information and solutions to achieve target outcomes in a streamlined way. A frictionless enterprise is core to success in delivering a perceptive, clean, relevant experience.

Future-proofing is the ability of an organization and its systems to execute continuous transformation that flexes with and adjusts to emerging requirements and changing compliance needs. Doing so reduces cost, time, and effort while increasing agility, efficiency, scalability, and, ultimately, profitability. All enterprise systems (including IT) are stable, secure, flexible, scalable, and learning-capable so they can grow at the pace your business requires, even if you don't know what that means in terms of functionality or operations.

Invisible, or ambient, technology is that which helps the customer or user get what they want in a way that is not intrusive, fast, seamless, and meets expectations on the go. People want to not be bothered with clunky technology, especially in a buying or service process. Technology needs to 'just work' in the background and it should be simple to use without a lot of training. Ambient means it is gently surrounding the user vs. being the center of attention.

Despite the name, **digital transformation** is not just about buying the latest and greatest technology. Instead, it is a process for improving customers' business outcomes and adding relevant value through streamlined processes, connected experiences and authentic relationships aided by technology. It means finding and adopting new ways of connecting people, processes, and data to enhance customer value delivery.

Digitizing systems and processes for every part of the business is vital to leverage staff capabilities. Just as (or even more) importantly, digital transformation moves business from systems of transactions to systems of engagement with personalized information, features, recommendations, and marketing. Systems of engagement means taking customer information for solving problems and meeting needs into actualizing solutions for them, and involving the (future) customer in that process. This creates and deepens the relationship which, over time, yields brand loyalty and advocacy.

Challenges Continued

Another pain point is that most of the organization off-loads the responsibility of attracting and building relationships to the marketing and sales teams when, in reality, it's everyone's responsibility. One of the ways to ensure every employee, regardless of role, knows this is to hold open marketing meetings to educate and inform employees about your organization's position, platform, presence, and marketing strategy in and for your market.

Organizational silos and information fiefdoms, where someone or a team controls access to knowledge for personal power, is a pain point that limits organizational growth. Where there are silos, there is also inefficient work, duplicated data, a fragmented view of the customer, and an 'us vs. them' mentality. Silos undermine corporate culture as the sense of community is diluted and departmental collaboration is diminished. The worst fallout from silos is that the customer experience cannot be seamless due to partial insight.

Another pain point is that implementation and delivery teams work by project, while marketers and sales work by real-time opportunities and deadlines. Marketers need things to happen quickly, sometimes on the fly, while implementation, delivery and service teams need to make sure every process is thorough and secure. In fact, it is this dynamic that contributes to the aforementioned silo effect.

Today's on-demand economy has surfaced challenges in customer (and user) expectations which affect the relationship journey. Customers expect innovation and solutions on their terms. Employees and users need to be at peak performance more than ever to meet assertive-to-be-competitive organizational targets; that need for convenience and speed can get to the point where they will use whatever tool gives them that functionality whether or not it is linked to marketing or sales systems. Without systems integration and the ability to flex with the rapid pace of change, it's challenging for marketers to create real-time, agile, personalized campaigns.

Additionally, there is an abundance of data but there can also be a lack of real insight when companies do not use their data effectively. This leads to poor decision-making, different lines of business drawing different conclusions, and a fractured brand.

Speaking of lack, the resources traditionally allocated to the marketing budget are often low to begin with when compared to the expected outcomes and, even more, are the first to be cut during lean times. This is an outdated paradigm that must adapt to today's business needs because, in the absence of marketing, there can be little growth for new business.

Then there is always the moving target on personas as buying decisions are now made by committee. The traditional decision-maker now has influencers and several people who each contribute their expertise to completing several tasks along the buying decision continuum: problem identification, solution requirements definition, options research and brainstorming, consensus-building, evaluation and finally purchase. There is a cascade effect that ripples throughout all the individuals involved in a buying decision, all of which are significant to the greater whole.

Additionally, business leaders who wear too many hats may be involved at multiple points in that process and may interpret marketing messages differently depending on the day.

Lastly, with customer connectivity, social proof, and the Internet of Things, there is an underlying theme of not having control over the brand story in every context in a dynamic business landscape. When every touchpoint with your brand can attract, reinforce or repel your brand story—a casual coffee shop conversation,or social media reference outside brand control, the best 'defense' is having clear messaging and a strong market presence. And, naturally, being responsive to what is stated publicly, taking swift action to remediate anything unsupportive to your brand, and, ideally, using language, tone, and voice to give your brand a relatable personality.

Altogether, where there is inflexibility, commitment to yesterday's practices, and analysis-paralysis for decision-making due to (potentially) all the factors above, the organization will experience stagnant or even negative results.

Next-level enterprise requires next-level marketing strategies and tactics, including messaging platforms that deliver relevant messaging in seconds, cognitive learning systems, hyper-personalized user experiences, intelligent bots. While, ultimately, it's about cultivating relationships, through delivering frictionless value, the process now relies on ambient technology, or systems that are unobtrusive, intelligent, and 'invisible' to the customer.

And all of it comes together in marketing, especially when there is a strategic framework in place.

Why People Buy Anything

After exploring the various pain points facing marketers, it's important to consider why people buy anything. There is the "know, like, and trust" factor of doing business, which is a subjective criteria that leads us to buy from our friends, acquaintances, and people we admire.

Then there is the heuristic impulse, which was a lesson in sales for me when I owned a niche boutique. One of my differentiators was my personal hand-selected merchandise that I would carefully display so customers could shop with a glance. And people didn't buy anything! Finally, I needed to get some cash flow going so I put up a table, piled everything on it to get it out of the way and separate from my regular inventory and I thought it was messy but made room for more beautiful displays.

As you might surmise, buyers would come into my store, walk past my ornate and deliberate displays, and head right for that heap of inventory on that table. They loved digging around—it was like a little discovery adventure. When they found something unique, they were invested in the process of finding it and bought it immediately. That is the heuristic impulse. It is subjective, personal, emotional, and intangible.

It's fairly common knowledge that emotion makes the decision to buy something, then logic validates it. If you've ever had a midnight craving for ice cream that, somehow, made it make sense for you to go out and get it, you've experienced this condition. When someone really wants something, they will find a way to rationalize their behavior to get it.

So, as marketers, is it helpful to understand how to call out the intangible value our company's solution(s) deliver? In a word, yes.

Twelve Intangible Benefits

Most companies don't realize how their brand value reaches in terms of intangible benefits to customers. These subtle benefits are powerful; they can surface opportunities, expand business relationships, and provide a new competitive edge in the market. And your organization might be delivering these intangible benefits right now without knowing it.

Understanding which of the twelve intangible benefits your company may be delivering could become a part of your brand promise and messaging. Just one of the following benefits demonstrates to your customers that you care and are thinking about how to help them get their desired outcomes.

1. Clarity

The more definition you can provide around the problems, issues, and challenges your customers face, the more credibility you have as a resource in addressing them. And bonus—the faster your customers can solve them because they now have focus. By helping your audience(s) gain clarity, which may happen in places where they might not even know they have confusion, you give language by which they can frame and share their problem(s). This is a first step toward solving them. Hot tip: the provider who can identify and name the issue is usually the one presumed to be able to fix it. The more clarity your company offers, the more business your company will likely attract.

2. Learn Faster

By supporting your customers in learning faster, you give them the ability to accelerate and compress their learning curve. By integrating new information into their unique situation faster, they naturally achieve their desired outcome faster. And that is a significant differentiator in business because time is a factor in generating revenues.

3. Design Their Outcome

We humans measure success by outcomes, meaning your customer needs to know what they want from working with you. By helping design the focused outcome of resolving an issue, your customer gains clarity, new possibilities, and a better idea about what they can get by hiring your company. Supporting your customers in determining exactly what they want is the first step of experiencing that outcome.

4. Upgrade Their Resources

Business is predicated on someone needing something that someone else can provide—including supporting customers in upgrading their resources. Your company might be helping your customers do their business better. Resources could be systems, technology, infrastructure, workflows, personnel, process… the end result of upgrading resources is found time through increased efficiency and productivity for your customer. And that impacts their bottom-line revenues.

5. Elevate Thinking

To transform anything to a next-level status, elevated thinking has to occur, meaning the exploration of new concepts, ideas, ways of doing things, business targets, business models, and more. Transformation is less about activities and more about the 'why' combined with strategy; when those are clearly articulated and aligned through more sophisticated thinking and a refined approach, a fresh and more expansive perspective can emerge. From that clarity, problem resolution and transformation occur naturally. Helping your customers elevate their thinking is a priceless benefit your company can offer.

6. Replace Outdated Paradigms

Paradigms are beliefs and ways of thinking that have become institutionalized as established routines over time. Paradigms can keep organizations trapped in historical patterns that no longer serve today's business targets. To reach, and then maintain, their desired new business outcomes, customers need to release and replace their limiting paradigms.

When your company helps customers see what's not working for them, and where the constraints in their thinking can be found, you create space for new potential to emerge. Fresh opportunities may emerge naturally as staff and leaders contribute their insights and perspectives. This particular benefit is significant and one that companies usually cannot achieve on their own. The release and replacing of paradigms means confronting the 'sacred cows' of an organization, meaning it is not easy (and just about impossible when a company tries to do it using only their insider's perspective). One example of a paradigm that changed an industry was the invention of the zipper which, at the time, was considered sinful due to the ease of disrobing. Today, zippers are a fashion staple—as is Velcro.

7. Transcend the Old

It is typically easier to stay in the status quo than to let go of it for something new, unknown, and unproven. When people are invested in preserving the comfort of the status quo, it can stall, block, or stop fresh momentum. It's important to let go of, "we've been doing it this way for so long," or, "we have already invested money in doing it that way." So, once again, the mantra of modern business: what worked then won't work now (or at least not the same way). A race cannot be won by looking backward; when you help your customer transcend the 'old' (beliefs, patterns, habits, routines, etc.) and face forward, they will gain new momentum and achieve faster results.

8. Expand Perception

The crux of transformation is perception because perception, or interpretation of circumstances, defines experience. Experience defines both issues and criteria for decision-making. So expanded perception means new awareness, by either adding new concepts, ideas, or solutions (aka, creative innovation) OR by taking away confusion, conflict, or complications (aka, creative destructionism), which creates the space to see new options.

9. Afford New Possibilities

Customers hire companies because they want a result they don't already have on their own. They want to go beyond their status quo, bust open their comfort zones, change things in a way that will predictably yield improved returns. In short, customers want a different future which motivates them to work with companies. They might not know exactly what they want, or know what's possible, or know how to leap the gap between where they are and where they want to be—and that's where the company comes in as the bridge. By discovering and naming the dynamics involved, and brainstorming new options, customers get excited about transformation. And, when your company demonstrates having the vision that can break their inertia, there is a natural presumption to see your company as the expert provider who can make it happen.

10. Advance Wholeness

When a system is whole, it is healthy. There is no need for conflict—problems, drama, chaos, anxiety, resistance, sabotage, struggle, etc.—because there is no longer a need to defend or justify a particular stance or position. Instead, all the parts of the system holistically work together. In any change process, including digital transformation, it is natural for people to get hooked into what they already know—it's their safe space even if it's dysfunctional or they want it to change.

However, when people can see there's a holistic approach in play with a bigger picture in mind, and especially when they are involved in the change process, they no longer need to defend what they thought they knew or have always done. They see it just doesn't make sense anymore because they have the context of the larger system as their reference point.

For example, marketing and sales is a core business ecosystem that often gets chopped up and compartmentalized to the point where each team is having different conversations. That creates a disconnect both internally and externally because it is fragmented, out of sync, and misaligned. Customers do not respond to piecemeal solutions. When your company is operating as a whole system and offering wholeness as a to benefit your customers when they work with your company, everyone wins.

11. Innovate Solutions

Innovation is about relevance, better ways of doing things, and having a competitive advantage. When done well, innovation can disrupt an entire market. So when your company solves problems in new ways, meaning with innovative solutions, your customers experience the power of possibility in action. Having new options can generate revitalized confidence. And it can be divisive when people want to bypass what's happening now and quantum leap into the new innovative future.

Conversely, there are also people who are invested in living from what they know and, so, will avoid new solutions. It's easier to allow and justify the status quo as efficient vs. having to learn something new that has yet to become a norm. Why? Because humans wear blinders to get through the day. If we didn't, we couldn't drive a car down the street without causing an accident. It is natural for us to filter out the familiar. A side effect of that particular survival skill is that, sometimes, we don't recognize what's happening that needs to change.

Here is an example that uses technology... people may not know their systems have aged beyond the point where it makes sense to maintain them, or that having such technical 'debt' (meaning investment in what's been purchased over the years) is jeopardizing or limiting functionality or security, or that having to piece data from three different systems into a spreadsheet really isn't so hard to do. When this paradigm is in place, innovation cannot occur. There is no awareness about the difference between cost (including opportunity cost) and investment. When your company can demonstrate the return on investment for innovating solutions, it can catapult companies into a whole new level of doing business.

12. Orient Around Truth

While customers want a new result, they often cannot see what is really happening. When your company helps customers recognize their reality, you give them the opportunity to see and orient around a truth that can upgrade their results. However, talking about and demonstrating a potentially unpopular and unknown truth can be challenging; compassion is crucial.

A harsh truth is something along the lines of "if you don't do this, your competitors will and your company will become obsolete"; by using different language, you can make the same point. "By upgrading your approach or innovating this solution or refining your system, your company can become an industry leader." Note the compassionate communication method articulated a specific solution path, along with the upside benefit of knowing and acting on that new truth. This way of speaking minimizes resistance while expressing the truth. When your company does that well with customers, your company will likely become known as an industry authority. Why? Because your loyal customers will want to share their success stories and that, naturally, cannot happen without referencing your company, using the language you used throughout their journey.

~ ~ ~ ~

Some of these intangible benefits may resemble or echo each other; at the same time, this is about subtle distinctions within your brand promise. Understanding which intangible benefit(s) your brand delivers can orient your company's messaging, positioning statements, selling conversations, industry articles, and more with a high degree of sophistication.

Invitation: I would love the opportunity to explore your digital brand promise, messaging, and intangible benefits. Whenever that seems it would be helpful to you, please drop me a line so we can schedule a call together.

Practical
Marketing Maneuvers

Now that we've covered the intangible benefits your organization may be delivering already, it's important to know who is going to care and, ultimately, become your customer. There are two aspects to this: 1) developing a profile of your ideal buyer(s) and 2) meeting the mental conversation already happening in your ideal buyer's mind.

Let's start by considering the mental conversation in your future customer's mind. For any buyer, there are five questions that need to be answered through your company's marketing copy and initiatives.

1. Who is this person talking to me and are they credible?
2. What is this solution, product, or service?
3. Why is it relevant to me? Why should I care?
4. How does it work?
5. How do I sign up?

Those are the five questions that any potential buyer is going to ask through any sales process, no matter the approach. As a marketer, you need to be able to address them. You have to show the value of your solution for that future customer, regardless of the sales approach. You have to look at how you're communicating value.

Each potential buyer will have different measures of value in their buying process according to what helps them deliver on their responsibilities. This is when thinking through buyer personas can be extremely helpful. It's also a step that many companies bypass in trying to drum up immediate business.

Persona Power

A buyer persona is an imaginary representative of your ideal customer. Personas help make it easier to understand the demographics and psychographics of your customer—like motivations, fears, challenges, preferences, questions, etc.—to customize content more effectively. By using insights from market research and your company's in-house data, like what your customers have consumed, their level of engagement in social media, their buying journey, what salespeople learn from working with them, and more, you can speak right to the heart of what will be relevant, timely, and compelling in terms of taking next action with your company. Companies will typically have at least two personas but may have many more.

In addition to the main buyer personas, you may want to develop influencer personas for those people who may be involved in the buying process. To determine which personas are needed, consider who is sponsoring your solution, who is your in-house champion for your solution, who is feeding information to influence the buying process, and who is the final approver—even if they are not the decision-maker. This could include such roles as the Chief Security Officer, the Chief Compliance Officer, the Marketing Manager, the Sales Director, the Corporate Trainer, the System Architect, the Chief Experience Officer or many, many others.

You can also create a negative buyer persona for buyers who do not fit your ideal customer profile. For example, you may not want to target students, researchers, or potential customers that are expensive to acquire with a projected low ROI (due to their potential churn factor, lack of brand loyalty, etc.). This helps you know who is not a good target audience for your marketing.

When promoting an offering, the same solution will be evaluated from various perspectives. For example, a CEO may want to know if your solution addresses today's issues while being adaptable to the future. A Chief Financial Officer (CFO) will want to make sure the solution is cost-effective and provides a good Return on Investment (ROI). A CIO will want to know how the solution fits into existing systems and what it will take to implement it. A CMO will want to know how the solution will promote and support relationships, marketing initiatives, and increasing brand visibility. So the same product will need to be considered from each persona's point of view to create messaging around your brand, offering, product, or service.

When creating buyer personas, you can consider a number of elements to build the profile as follows.

Title	Median Salary	Average Age
Gender	Purchase Drivers	Wants
Skills	Needs	Environment
Beliefs	Attitudes	Motivators
Pain Points	Frustrations	Fears
Media Consumed	Communities	Resolution Point

While most of those terms are likely understood, there are a couple that may need further explanation. Purchase drivers typically means which of the following is most important in a buying decision: price, features, brand, design, or innovation. Media Consumed means how that persona does research for solutions and where they are already looking for information—social media, tv news, magazines, newspapers, online forums, etc. Communities include professional associations, forums, clubs, groups, or any other collective group of people that may influence their process. And Resolution Point means the one question that will help that persona make a buying decision.

For example, using the very rough personas above, here are points of resolution to demonstrate what that buyer wants to know so they can make an affirmative purchasing decision.

> **CEO:** Will this purchase help us achieve our goals faster, easier, effectively, efficiently, and/or deliver greater value?
>
> **CFO:** Will this purchase provide maximum ROI, reduce our potential liabilities, and/or increase our assets?
>
> **CIO:** Will this purchase increase our capabilities, integrate well, stabilize our environment, be secure, and future-proof our technology?
>
> **CMO:** Will this purchase help us generate demand, attract new buyers, and retain current customers?

Beyond that, there are the four voices of copywriting, which frame even more subtleties in understanding and speaking to your future buyers.

Four Voices of Copywriting

I felt like I needed to include this section because, even when you identify your personas, including influencers, you still need to be able to address their psychographics through narrative. That is, people tend to read copy through their primary filters of perception; as a marketer, you need to be able to speak on all four levels for website copy, general campaigns, marketing initiatives and more.

THE FOUR VOICES OF COPYWRITING

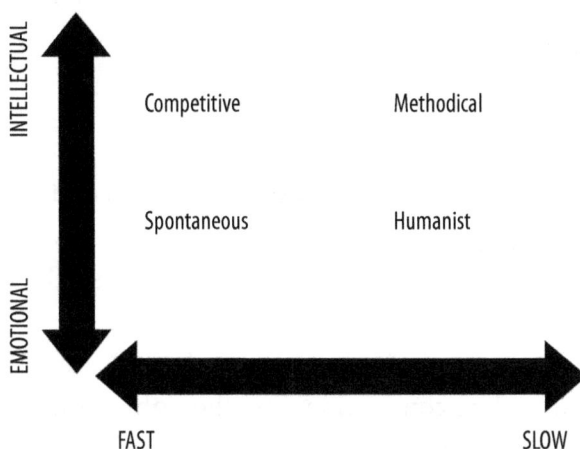

The four voices of copywriting include Competitive, Spontaneous, Methodical, and Humanist.

The left side of this simple chart are the fast decision-makers; the right side are slower in their decision-making. The top of this chart is more intellectual in terms of being analytical, while the bottom row people tend to be more emotional in their decision-making. As a quick reference, if you are a Star Trek fan, you'll recognize Scotty (Competitive), Spock (Methodical), Bones (Humanist) and Captain Kirk (Spontaneous).

One of the most fascinating exercises I did early in my career was to write the same website copy completely for each of these four voices. I had four totally different website pages—for the same offer! A good copywriter will know how to blend all four voices into a single offer.

Below is a quick reference for each of the four voices so you can see the differences and possibly even evaluate your current marketing content accordingly.

1. Competitive

Competitive buyers use a combination of intuition and critical thinking, can be a bit skeptical, tend to follow formulas, want precision, 'show me' copy and visuals and to have control so they can make quick logical decisions.

They are competent, curious, enjoy challenges, are goal-oriented, follow tasks through to completion, find the right place and then look for a reason to stay there. They are motivated, image conscious, not hedonistic (impulsive), and intense. They can carry grudges, are planners in advance, and like to save time. Once they are clear, they decide fast; often they can start as Competitive and go Methodical.

Needs: they do not want to scroll on a website. Price is not a leading factor in their decision-making. They do want big headlines, bullet points, to answer 'what's in it for me?', and clear benefits. They ask, 'will this make me more credible / look better / keep me achieving / have a recipe for a better life?'

Points of Resolution: Newness or leading-edge quality of solution, appeal to others, brand presence, guarantees, ratings by others, endorsements.

2. Methodical

Methodical people are good at sensing or judging circumstances, situations, and solutions. They are the "adult" in most situations. They care about infrastructure and the finer details. While they are emotional in their decision-making, they tend to make slow decisions backed by their analytical thinking.

They are typically prepared, have and like facts, specifics, and details. They are logical, appreciate documentation of truth, and having organization and timelines. They do not like a personal touch or irresponsibility. They will look for what's wrong with an offer.

Needs: they want to know the fine print before they sign. Need details, to know the process, be able to plan ahead, get proof the solution works (including social proof and warranties), and guarantees.

Points of Resolution: See how the solution connects in their existing process or framework. They want to see process, case studies, specifications, samples, competing solutions, and standards (of progress, success, expectations, etc.).

3. Spontaneous

Spontaneous buyers are good at sensing and perceiving. They tend to like action and adventure, they are best in crisis and, predictably, make fast decisions (which means they need to know how to return things or reverse impulse buys later).

They live in the moment, don't scroll or research deeply. They are sensory, flexible, and get easily distracted by bright / shiny objects. They are on a personal quest for impact. They want big statements and excitement. They do not like a lot of details and have FOMO (a fear of missing out).

Needs: they want to know how to get 'it' quickly. They want to be able to customize, get help in narrowing their choices, and, most importantly, to know it will let them enjoy their life more.

Points of Resolution: They are attracted to color, ease of use, free and fast delivery. Size matters—the bigger, the better. They like discounts, a good price, and a generous return policy.

4. Humanist

Humanists intuit and feel their way into a decision. They want ever-deeper intimacy and always honesty. They are empathic, spiritual, and take care of others. They seek what is significant and has potential. It is about relationships, community, and belonging for these buyers.

They are emotional, put others first, and often find it hard to receive. They are creative, value relationships, fear separation and follow through where they are emotionally invested. They are good listeners, value acceptance and freedom. They are loyal over the long term.

Needs: they like referrals, trust symbols, stories, testimonials, connection points with community, to belong.

Points of Resolution: Humanists want credibility, trustworthiness, and authority through people's experience—testimonials, reviews, case studies, success stories. And they want to experience a feeling of ownership.

You can see how the four voices can affect marketing messaging. We'll get to that—first, let's talk Value Proposition because this is another critical piece that is often overlooked in the desire to get to market faster.

Value Proposition

Essentially, your company's value proposition is the brand promise made visible. It is what I like to call your DNA, or Distinct Niche Advantage. It is the differentiator that makes your company stand out against the competition. It is the unique attraction factor that makes it difficult for others to compete against your company.

Most companies focus on the 'how' of their solution vs. their 'why'; the why makes a more compelling selling point than the how. A good value proposition is strong enough to compel a customer to saying 'yes' to taking action with a company. It answers the question: 'why should I buy your solution vs. any other?'

There are two types of value proposition: one for the offer and one for the buyer. Both are gateways to trust. By using positioning statements related to the value proposition, the buyer enters and progresses through the ecosystem via micro-yes's. "Yes, I choose to… notice that ad, click on that ad, give my email address, read that content, have a phone call, share with my team, etc.'

Interestingly, the value proposition will vary slightly by persona to address their goal(s), motivation(s) and experience with the buying process they are currently working. You know where there is a value proposition in action because it's where the buyer is being asked to do something. In other words, a buyer will only click on, download, read, watch, or do something that offers them value… which means that value should be derived from the value proposition. So, 'enter your name and email to download this whizbang report' means that piece is somehow relevant to the value proposition and perceived value to the future customer.

All sales begin through marketing; marketing optimizes thought sequences while sales personalizes solutions and handles the transaction. The value proposition needs to be framed in the language and logic of the buyer vs. company language or logic.

As a quick aside, sequencing your buyer's thoughts means that you are clarifying the promise of what they will get with your solution, painting the picture of their future as a result of your solution, providing proof that others have experienced success with your solution, and amping up the 'pull' factor about what they need to believe in order to allow their vision and desire to convert to taking action. The goal of marketing is to progress the buyer's mindset naturally and easily through what they need to know to make a clear decision.

Now, to help identify your Value Proposition, answer the following questions.

- What need does your solution meet or problem does your solution solve?
- In what ways is your solution superior to similar available solutions?

- What did your previous customers really buy from you? (Peace of mind, get more time, things flow easier, etc.)
- Why should your potential customers trade their time, that they will never get back, to engage with your enterprise? (Think benefits.)
- What is the value exchange that happens between your customers and your organization?
- What is the positive end result of your business strategy?

Here is a simple statement you can use when articulating your Value Proposition.

If I am a (buyer / customer persona), why should I be interested in your solution(s) rather than any others?

The language you use here needs to be concise, based on customer perspective, and unique. If another company could post it and it would make sense, you need to go further to find your differentiator.

Positioning Statements

One more technique to be aware of when it comes to value propositions... positioning statements. Your marketing strategy depends on good positioning.

Positioning statements are nuances of the value proposition and are designed to speak to a particular persona or marketplace audience. One value proposition could generate several positioning statements.

Positioning statements are tailored to a unique persona, demonstrating understanding of that persona. Positioning statements consider what your ideal buyer persona sees in the marketplace as influences (including competitor information) so they can make a more informed decision. Positioning statements focus on what is relevant, practical, and valuable to that persona (because all else is distraction).

Here is a simple process to write your positioning statements.

1. Choose a buyer persona for your focus with a positioning statement.

2. Create a list of needs that your buyer persona has which your solution can meet. (You may already have this identified when you created your buyer persona.)

3. List your solution's benefits that distinctly meet these needs.

4. Use the above information to complete this sentence: 'When this buyer thinks of my company's (<u>solution</u>), I want them to think: _____.'

5. Refine your positioning statement to make it clear, simple, and consistent with the rest of your marketing positioning.

6. Use this positioning statement for marketing initiatives relevant to this buyer. Make sure your colleagues, staff, and leadership (especially the sales team) also know the positioning statement so they can reinforce it in conversations.

Marketing Hooks

Just like when fishing, you need to have interesting bait to attract attention. This is where understanding your market and ideal buyers becomes vital.

A marketing hook is different from a positioning statement in that the positioning statement frames the offer and the marketing hook is the enticing intro to it. A marketing hook is the attention-grabber that gets noticed and begins the relationship with your ideal customer.

Think of a marketing hook as a tease, a sample, a mental appetizer that attracts attention to your marketing messages and company. The hook should give your buyers just enough taste to leave them wanting more—it's not a whole offer. When people take the hook, they give you permission to follow up and market more to them.

To make your marketing hook memorable:

- Announce something new.
- Surprise the buyer to get attention (by using contrary viewpoints, using commands, telling the future, sounding an alarm, etc.).
- Use emotion, exclamations (sparingly), or bold statements.
- Promise a benefit or a solution.
- Doing something different (like offering a free phone chat or membership).
- Offering valuable information (such as a content asset: white paper, special report, checklist, top 10 list, etc.).

Message Mapping

Now that you have your customer experience strategy designed, your intangible benefits articulated, your buyer personas identified, your value proposition and positioning statements in place, and you are aware of the four voices to help communicate with your personas, you need to know what you are going to say in terms of messaging.

A quick caveat: entire books have been dedicated to the topics I'm covering in a few pages! I'm touching on highlights of these topics because it seems appropriate for this kind of book and because there are times when my comprehensive thinking demands I be as thorough as possible.

Here is my philosophy on marketing messages: smart messages attract smart customers. A smart message distills direct thoughts: how to meet needs, anticipate goals, share the vision, and teach people (not ideas or probabilities). The smarter the message, the more educated (smarter) your audience(s).

Obviously, good marketing messages are the foundation of your brand's success. Messaging occurs on three levels (the first two can happen simultaneously):

1. The overall market or industry,

2. Specific people which can be categorized into personas, or avatars, for simplicity in communication, and,

3. Finding the right thing to say at the right time.

Messaging is the art of defining narrative conversation to your ideal persona(s) and the form you will use to share it. It is also the bridge between positioning and actually creating content.

The purpose of a marketing message is to serve as a blueprint that sequences communications with your audience(s) and guides development of tactics including content marketing, web content, email marketing, event collateral and live sales conversations. Marketing messages deliver your intentional customer experience to drive marketplace visibility, thought leadership, and generate leads and upsell opportunities. It's important to measure incremental results through key metrics and analytics so you know what's working with your audience(s).

As a quick refresh, your Value Proposition is your brand promise, the end result of your work in a given market. Positioning statements are about targeted benefits to a specific persona(s) or audience(s) and can include the contrast between your solution and your competitors. A message is what you want to say to a specific persona(s) using various techniques like: storytelling, thought leadership, or video marketing. All three need to work in concert for effective messaging.

A well-crafted message will highlight your unique benefits, target your persona(s) / audience(s), support your mission, and often include a call to action. An effective marketing message is:

- An insight that captures existing persona beliefs, illustrating the problem or unmet need your solution addresses,
- A benefit that articulates the appealing and distinctive promise your solution offers, providing the reason buyers would become your customers (vs. the competition's), and,
- A 'reason-to-believe' that supports or explains why customers can believe the promised benefit(s) will be delivered as their experience.

Essentially, there are nine 'sales' marketing messages should make:

1. Attention (as in, get it—break through the marketplace 'noise'),
2. Readership (so the person consumes it),
3. Benefit (how it is relevant to the persona(s)),
4. Credibility (your brand's authority through social proof, brand presence, and voice),
5. Uniqueness (your solution is not available elsewhere),
6. Value (that the customer gets back more than they pay),
7. Safety (their info is protected, you have guarantees, they can contact you easily),
8. Convenience (easy to understand and take action), and,
9. Now (sense of urgency to compel taking action).

Your narrative should support your brand through such pieces as:

- Website Copy / Landing Pages,
- White Papers,

- E-books,
- Executive Papers,
- Articles and Blogs,
- Product Briefs,
- Brochures,
- Case Studies,
- Presentations,
- Thought Leadership Pieces,
- Video Scripts,
- Social Media,
- And more.

The most likely scenario is that a combination of the above will best meet the needs of your audience(s); the right combination is determined by your existing results, desired outcome(s), and content strategy.

One more point: messages should be deliberately crafted to meet each persona strategically and tactically. Strategic messaging expresses the "why?" and "how?", while tactical messaging expresses the details of the strategy by answering the "what?" and "where?"

For example:

CFO Strategic: This solution is cost-effective and provides a good return on investment (ROI).

CFO Tactical: You should see an 8% return in 30 days as determined by monitoring new pipeline opportunities that convert more rapidly into new business.

One important type of message is what I call an Audio Logo, which is a short, clear, memorable phrase targeted right to a particular persona.

(Who—be descriptive) hires / works with / gets value from (company name) to do (what / your solution) so they can (benefits).

Example:

Visionary enterprises hire me to develop digital transformation strategies so they can design and deliver better customer and user experiences, increase audience engagement, and provide greater value as a leader in their market.

~ ~ ~ ~

You might find the form and some of the words shift to accommodate the person / audience you are talking to in the moment. You can also adapt this formula to different products and/or services.

There is something I call 'core messaging', which is the single unifying business storyline of your company, which should inform any other stories or information your audience(s) cares about when it comes to your brand or even your industry. Several types of content can come from a single business storyline. Your business storyline(s) should always reflect your core messaging. Stories should be compelling, evocative, memorable, and real.

Marketers need to tell a story that has impact, actionable frameworks, and a compelling call to action. Following is a formula for telling a solid business story; if you study writing at all, you will recognize this three-part formula in books and movies as well.

Challenge: Something has had to be overcome.

Action: People carry out actions (specific tangible things, like purchase your company's solution) to react to the challenges.

Transformation: The world (and the hero) changes because of their actions.

Example:

Enterprises have gotten so efficient with their marketing that they have left people out of the equation. By using a strategic approach to initiating digital transformation and humanizing the brand, staff and leadership are involved for organization-wide upgrades in processes, protocols, and personal empowerment in cultivating relationships. As a result, the company benefits from happier customers AND employees, which means relationships last longer, thus a reduced need to 'recruit' new business and staff, as well as deeper levels of work with customers.

~ ~ ~ ~

One of the more comprehensive services I offer my clients is creating a Message Map that considers all these elements: value proposition, big four (vision, mission, values, purpose), positioning statement(s), core message storyline, personas, audio logo, solution benefits, customer benefit, features, emotional state, and tagline.

This becomes the blueprint by which all content emerges from... including the customer experience via their systems, their go-to-market strategy, topics for hub (or central) content pieces, ancillary content (for specific channels, for example), competitive positioning, and more. When you put a Message Map together, it can be illuminating as to why a company is experiencing certain results (like, traffic, types of customers, requests for solutions, etc.). It's one of my most favorite things to do for that reason!

So knowing what your content is actually communicating is key to more effectively driving leads, increasing revenue, and building relationships with your customers. Following are some things you can do on your own to get a handle on your company's messaging.

- **Content / Asset Audit:** A content audit is not about the data but, instead, is a qualitative review of your existing assets to evaluate against your brand presence, voice and tone, visual style and more. Taking it one step further, throughout the audit process, it is noted where there is an opportunity to create new content for your customers' benefit.

Note: your company's messaging or impact through narrative could change over time in response to pacing with dynamic marketplace needs. Be sure to revisit your company's marketing, from the top down, at least annually to ensure everything still represents your enterprise.

- **Ideation:** This is the process of finding relevant, valuable topics that will resonate with your target audience(s). It includes having a paradigm framework for what your customers believe and what you want them to believe as well as keyword research.

- **Content Marketing Strategy:** All content should move the consumer to having more knowledge that is beneficial to engaging with your brand and understanding your solutions. The content marketing strategy typically orients around a 'hub' piece of content, such as a white paper or video series.

- **Content Editorial Calendar:** Developing a 12-month editorial calendar to structure the development and deployment of content pieces topically, chronologically and cross-channel (for delivery). Both the audience and the delivery channel must be considered, as well as optimal timing, against current events, upcoming events, time of year (like holidays). It also must be flexible to take advantage of emerging opportunities.

Altogether, this should be more than you never asked for to jumpstart messaging and marketing initiatives that evoke audience emotion and translate into action.

How Marketing
Can Lead Transformation

Business is about delivering value; strategy is about how to do it with the least amount of stress for the greatest return on investment. Sometimes marketers have the unique vantage point to ask the questions that provide perspective, insight, and competitive realities. This, essentially, finds the entry point to spearheading digital transformation.

Digital Transformation Readiness

The first way to know your organization needs digital transformation is if you're waiting for an obvious and clear answer. In that case, you're probably already behind what's needed to be competitive. Your company's goal for initiating digital transformation is to upgrade proactively—systems, skills, workflows, technologies, etc.—to position and be ready to take advantage of new opportunities as they emerge. Equally as important, your company needs to pace and project customer needs, wants, and demands, then be able to deliver it effectively, efficiently, and without friction.

The rise of the IoT, where digital devices are creating access and connection around the clock, is giving way to the 'Internet of Me' where customers drive business. As a result, companies need to change how they approach their business and how they leverage technology. Groceries are available on-demand around the clock with a click, a smartwatch is the only tool needed to order a car ride, watch the latest movie release, or to broadcast an email, and global conferences are hosted through virtual reality devices. Digital transformation is not an 'if' decision for enterprises but a 'when'—because your customers are demanding it.

There are a number of signals that indicate it's time for your company to consider a digital transformation process. (See the 'Symptoms That Precede Need for Digital Transformation' chart in a previous chapter.) While presented previously as symptoms, here is a quick refresh from a purely marketing perspective.

> **First,** look at what your customers are experiencing. When your customers aren't experiencing a smooth and seamless positive relationship with your company that keeps them going and growing, that's a good barometer of what's happening for your long-term business sustainability.

> **Second,** similarly, when your workflows are clunky or cumbersome, if your users and employees aren't quite connecting, if you have silos within your company, if communication is stunted or stagnant, then it's time to evaluate the investment in a digital transformation initiative.

> **Third,** look at what's happening in your industry. This isn't about competition in the way you might think; you want to be aware of what's happening in the industry because that's what your current and future customers are seeing. Then assess with straightforward, direct, and relentless honesty, how your brand measures up. Consider your brand presence, your messaging, your business model, your sales process, your workflows, your infrastructure… everything as it relates to what customers will experience to see what your company needs to upshift.

Following are questions that can reveal additional indicators that it's time to consider initiating a digital transformation journey in your company.

- Are your ideal customers, market, or industry having conversations that are different from your company's positioning, brand promise, or solutions?

- Is your company pacing industry growth in terms of best practices, technologies, solutions, systems, infrastructure, brand presence, growth strategies or anything else that is becoming a new standard or expectation in your industry?

- Are your audiences (both external and internal) enjoying a frictionless, integrated, tech-invisible experience at all touchpoints with your company?

- Are your online reviews or social media channels signaling something your company could be doing better or where there are unmet needs in your market?

- When there are lost business opportunities, does your company interview those lost customers to learn why your company was not chosen as the solution provider? If yes, does your company take that information seriously and adapt accordingly where warranted?

- Does your company hold interviews with exiting employees? If yes, when there is negative feedback, does your company take that information seriously and act on their recommendations where warranted?

- Do your salespeople regularly debrief what they're hearing in the field? Do your sales and marketing teams tell the same stories?

- Do business and tech teams work collaboratively and in alignment?

- Are your employees likely to be open to cross-functional team communication, workflows, collaboration, and projects-especially in remote or virtual workspaces?

- Does your staff know that, regardless of their responsibilities, they are a customer service agent first?

This is a crucial insight. Every staff member and leader need to prioritize customer concerns, wants, and needs, whether or not their role is publicly customer-facing. Customer-centricity and deepening relationships with empathy, sincere connection, and meaningful relevance are not just buzzwords. Humanizing your brand experience, then personalizing it, is the only overarching strategy your company has for sustainable business. This means having real conversations, being aware of their behaviors and preferences, and developing processes, workflows, and solutions accordingly is how your company can deliver value today while forecasting future strategies to be ready for conversations 'tomorrow.'

In terms of right timing for initiating digital transformation, the best way is to ask the people in your business ecosystem. "Is there anything we can do better?" "What is the quality of your experience with our company?" "Do you have recommendations on how we can improve?" The gravity of the answers, along with the degree of positive impact by creating change, will help determine the urgency of getting started.

There are various triggers that can initiate a digital transformation process, such as requiring a particular business outcome, accommodating regulatory compliance, an adaptation in business model, implementing a new innovation, market conversations, or even choosing to work with a vendor experienced in guiding, supporting, or implementing a digital transformation journey. Any limitation or constraint that limits your company's ability to deliver customer value or constrains your company's viability is a prompt to do something different.

You should know digital transformation never really ends... because it gets your company to the ever-evolving next best level of frictionless operations, future-proof technology, and customer-centric solutions and services.

Altogether, marketers can be pivotal in helping a company see what is needed for sustainable competitive advantage, positioning, streamlined systems, and fresh business opportunities with customers.

What Change Looks Like

In the beginning, change looks like chaos. Adjusting to it requires a learning curve. You will encounter unexpected barriers and problems that need solving. Digital transformation implies it's about technology, and technology is a beautiful thing. It does amazing stuff, but the reality is that it's powered by people. There is a synergy there. When people aren't on board with the change, it's important to look at what's going on—where's the resistance? What do people need? Is it about awareness? Do they need the bigger picture or to expand their thinking or be reassured they will have job security?

Visionary leadership is also a huge factor in that leaders need to get out in the field and see what's going on: talk to people, go to events, read magazines and articles, watch videos, or listen to podcasts. Remember, the CEO typically mandates a digital transformation process, while the CIO needs to make it happen operationally, and the CMO is responsible for the strategy that puts results in motion.

There are many different ways to support the changes that occur with digital transformation throughout a company; one of the most overlooked is simply having a strategic action plan for it. This plan should detail how your company will share information and progress updates, who is responsible for what actions, what the process is re: business units or teams, the meetings that will be needed, what predicted pockets of resistance that will likely need to be addressed, and more.

The most important lynchpin of any change process is to communicate in multiple ways, to different audiences, to every part of the organization about current status, what's coming next, and what people should expect along the way. In the absence of information, people make up stories. They try to fill in the gaps on their own. Then they share that with their colleagues. And, ultimately, that means doing damage control after the fact for what was originally preventable fiction. So hold a kickoff, regular employee meetings, send e-updates, have an open door policy, proactively check with staff and leaders to take a temperature on the process, and anything else that will ensure people have information about the status and changes for and throughout the process.

There are times when people are so invested in doing a good job as they've always done it that they are afraid to change because they fear losing power, status, or job security. Even more, when people don't have access to the bigger vision and larger context, they will keep going with what they know to do to keep the proverbial lights on vs. trying something new.

To the degree there is a reaction is to the degree where a shift is occurring *and* where information needs to be shared. Continuously and proactively communicating and listening are the two best ways to facilitate digital transformation.

Growth Requires Business Strategy

Growth initiatives need the framework of strategy or they will not gain traction. Ideas without strategy stay a vision, while strategy without action is simply a concept.

There are a number of factors that affect growth, from the competition to new technologies, from dynamic customer conversations to shifts in the market, and much more. Strategy considers the moving parts with a future-thinking perspective to play out different scenarios, evaluate probabilities, brainstorm potential ways to leap the gap between today and tomorrow, then discerns where the greatest business impact—positive or negative—is so your company can make decisions for informed action.

Strategy also turns industry disruption and challenges into growth opportunities. Daniel Burrus, Disruption Innovation Expert, would call this being an "anticipatory organization." Consider medical clinics located inside retail and grocery stores, 3D printing and manufacturing, lockboxes for pizza pickup, the coronavirus causing more remote working… virtually anything that happens creates an ending that is needed to have a new beginning in some way. Strategy takes that change and ensures it has the shortest path to grow into profit or positive impact.

So business growth is always good, right? Wrong.

Efficient business growth that delivers effective, meaningful, and relevant customer value for their satisfaction and expected results and, ideally, which makes a profit is always good. Should you need to make a business case for growth, be sure to use credibility in documenting the bigger 'why' it matters, get buy-in from internal champions, and identify the needed funding sources as infrastructure for presenting your transformational business growth idea.

How to Know Marketing Strategy Is Needed

Strategy is a vital element in the success of any company because it makes the most of resources, and reduces stress, in reaching business targets. Marketing strategy optimizes marketing investments. Following are the top ten indicators that can help your organization know whether a marketing strategy should be a priority.

1. **Unclear purpose.** Your organization's reason for being, and the positive difference it makes for its audiences, must be known, concisely stated, and compelling.

2. **Unknown customers.** Your organization needs to know who your ideal customers are, as well as their buying process, motivations, challenges, interests, preferences, influences, and more, to ensure your brand experience adds relevant and meaningful value at every touchpoint with them.

3. **Lost leadership position.** When new companies and competitors gain visibility, authority, and market share, analysis is needed to strategize a plan to (re)establish your company's leadership position.

4. **Value proposition.** Your organization must have a statement that defines key differentiators and approach to solving customer problems and delivering value.

5. **Unknown market share.** It is essential to know who your company best serves as your ideal customers, how visible your brand is with them, and what other company(ies) they might perceive as leading your industry.

6. **Fragmented systems.** If your systems, processes, protocols, teams, or workflows are not integrated, that fragmentation could result in missed opportunities, overlooked revenue sources, insufficient insights from data, and more. Integration is not optional for business today.

7. **Gap in skills or staff.** Not having the right (or enough) employees trained and in place, or the marketing team not having an appropriate budget to achieve targets, will constrict results from marketing initiatives.

8. **Insufficient tech.** In the case of aging IT infrastructure, a reliance on manual processing operationally, or not being able to measure real-time performance and/or results, your company likely has redundant effort and wasted resources.

9. **Lack agility.** Your organization needs to set the pace, tone, and/or expectations of your market on the go; when that is not happening, or your company does not have the agility to

do so in real-time, it's a '911' to plan and take action accordingly with urgency.

10. **Marketing is undervalued.** Your organization needs to optimize all marketing insights, actions, campaigns, events, communications, and opportunities. When marketing is undervalued or under-resourced, it is not possible to reach new audiences or keep the brand relevant in the market. There is significant opportunity cost as a consequence of minimizing marketing strategies and activities.

~ ~ ~ ~

Marketing is the engine that drives organizational growth. Strategy is how to optimize resources and systematically address factors that could negatively impact the bottom line. Together, regardless of the channel, format, campaign, platform, or location, digital marketing and associated strategies are the growing edge for leadership, authority, and long-term sustainability by reaching customers where they metaphorically live—online.

Having read all this, how is your company doing in terms of understanding, valuing, and applying B2B marketing strategy to your brand promise and communications? When an organization is too far ahead of its reality with its self-perception, or is disconnected from its audiences, or considers strategy as a myth, there are going to be challenges in business growth as well as opportunity cost. Such an organization can be left behind in their industry, forced to run faster and harder just to try to keep up, much less claim industry leadership.

A comprehensive digital transformation initiative can take all of those factors into consideration when operationalizing next-level strategies. Where your company is now is the raw fuel that will power future success. Let your company's current circumstances be a launchpad while strategy the ignition system and marketing the fuel for growth.

Summary

The heart of business growth is relationships. Creating and cultivating relationships are the heart of marketing. Strategic marketing goes beyond tasks, activities, and campaigns to connect the dots between brand experience and customer engagement with less stress and most efficient use of resources. Digital transformation is the process that upshifts systems, processes, and people into a more human-centric focus where relationships and their experiences inform the business model and, ultimately, revenues. Essentially, relationships yield revenues.

This book has covered a broad range of topics synthesized into (hopefully) cohesive order to make it easier to understand and make the case for digital transformation in your organization.

In the context of the digital economy, which is the Experience Economy, it's an exciting time to be in marketing. Timelines are compressed, launches and campaigns happen with faster iterations, data provides insights with a click, collaboration is becoming more streamlined as silos break down and digital workspaces become customary, connecting with audiences outside the business ecosystem happens directly through social media channels, and the path to success is clearly known due to feedback from all touchpoints. The question is whether an organization is willing to adapt accordingly and, in most cases, initiate and/or continue digital transformation.

The considerations of doing so are numerous; some of what organizations will encounter and need to address include the following.

- Identifying and then dismantling silos of information, teams, roles, and expectations for greater integration and cross-functional collaboration.
- Pacing, and ideally leading, the market, particularly when it comes to competitors. Agility is a critical success factor in retaining industry leadership.
- Honoring customer data privacy concerns, needs, and regulations while personalizing brand experiences.
- Aligning marketing messaging and sales conversations, especially where seasoned staff (with entrenched habits) are concerned.
- Addressing any resistance to the changes that will occur in a way that is straightforward and non-confrontational.
- Ensure staff has the right skills, training, and tools to optimize peak performance.

The good news is that by having the vision and the courage to handle the above, and more, there are just as many—if not more—benefits to the organization.

- Operational infrastructure and processes revolve around relationships, delivering value, and customer expectations.
- Technology becomes frictionless, more agile, and invisible to audiences who simply get what they want when they want it the way they want it.
- Messaging is relevant, practical, timely, and meaningful to ideal customers.
- Brand presence, reputation management, and market visibility gain in-house support and resources rather than being a by-product of marketing activities.

- Team collaboration across functionality, aligned with company values, which uplevels the corporate culture.
- Partnerships, strategic alliances, and joint ventures work cohesively to support the market with a sense of 'coopetition' vs. competition.
- Innovation in learning, adapting, generating solutions, and upgrading systems for continuous improvement becomes the norm.
- Engagement with customers happens as part of everyday activities via an omnichannel presence which builds community, trust, and loyalty vs. as a by-product of sales or service calls.
- Expanding into new markets becomes easier with clear brand positioning, presence, and perception-shaping.
- Strategy enables activities and campaigns that happen with right resources, in right timing, in the right order, with the right staff for the right audiences.

Altogether, holistic, systemic changes happen as a result of digital thinking and strategic frameworks. Customers—both external and internal—are assured value and a quality experience at every touch-point. Organizations reduce expenses and generate more revenues.

Whether a company is a start-up or established, uses an online or traditional office structure, is an industry leader or not yet, digital transformation and strategic marketing to upshift the brand experience is the only sustainable advantage in today's business landscape. To not invest in either means enduring opportunity costs in lost business, redundant efforts, extra expense, and other resources organizations cannot afford to waste.

The most significant influencer on business growth, outside of customer expectations, is having a strategy in place and being willing to accommodate to changing conditions. Everything else will sort itself out—and you'll know it's happening by the degree of success your organization has over the long term.

As I said in the beginning of this book, I am a born transformationalist. What I know is that those who do not keep up with evolution get left behind by it. By embracing and proactively inviting change, whether an organization or a person, life thrives.

It is my greatest desire that my thoughts here have given you insights, clarity, and a reason to take new action in your organization. I'd love to hear about it. Please send me an email and let me know at **support@savvyx.com**.

And in case you feel moved to share this book with someone, know that you are being a catalyst in their world. It could make all the difference for them. On behalf of both that future person and myself, thank you in advance.

About the Author

LYNN SCHEURELL, B2B digital transformation specialist, speaker, and author, facilitates fresh results from current circumstances to actualize business potential.

People assign various descriptions to the value Lynn brings to situations and relationships: catalyst for change, results accelerator, innovator, out-of-the-box visionary, big-picture analytical thinker, positive energy, being a 'possibilitarian'.

Having been an internet marketer since 1998, she grew her skills with the emerging digital economy. Formalizing her experience into being a strategist, brand development expert, and copywriter, she has worked with companies in multiple verticals on various initiatives related to digital transformation. The key to success—always—is buy-in and support from the people involved in the transformation process.

Her intention is to make a positive difference, solve problems, offer compelling clarity, and help people live happier professionally. She believes happy people make things happen, in which case we all win.

Specialties:

- Digital Transformation
- Analytical Thinking
- Brand Development & Strategy
- Content & Digital Marketing
- Customer Experience Mapping
- Thought Leadership Platform-Building
- Copywriting
- Book Ghostwriter
- Strategic Planning
- Group Facilitation
- Storyteller

You can reach her through **SavvyX.com** or on LinkedIn: **linkedin.com/in/lynnscheurell/**.

Download Your Free Digital Transformation Blueprint

A downloadable PDF that breaks down the five steps of developing and delivering Savvier brand experiences.

Get It NOW at
savvyx.com/blueprint/

www.ingramcontent.com/pod-product-compliance
Lightning Source LLC
Chambersburg PA
CBHW071710210326
41597CB00017B/2419